Extreme
Programming
Explored

The XP Series

Kent Beck, Series Advisor

Extreme Programming, familiarly known as XP, is a discipline of business and software development that focuses both parties on common, reachable goals. XP teams produce quality software at a sustainable pace. The practices that make up "book" XP are chosen for their dependence on human creativity and acceptance of human frailty.

Although XP is often presented as a list of practices, XP is not a finish line. You don't get better and better grades at doing XP until you finally receive the coveted gold star. XP is a starting line. It asks the question, "How little can we do and still build great software?"

The beginning of the answer is that, if we want to leave software development uncluttered, we must be prepared to completely embrace the few practices we adopt. Half measures leave problems unsolved to be addressed by further half measures. Eventually you are surrounded by so many half measures that you can no longer see that the heart of the value programmers create comes from programming.

I say, "The beginning of the answer …" because there is no final answer. The authors in the XP Series have been that and done there, and returned to tell their story. The books in this series are the signposts they have planted along the way: "Here lie dragons," "Scenic drive next 15 km," "Slippery when wet."

Excuse me, I gotta go program.

Titles in the Series

Extreme Programming Applied: Playing to Win, Ken Auer and Roy Miller

Extreme Programming Examined, Giancarlo Succi and Michele Marchesi

Extreme Programming Explained: Embrace Change, Kent Beck

Extreme Programming Explored, William C. Wake

Extreme Programming in Practice, James Newkirk and Robert C. Martin

Extreme Programming Installed, Ron Jeffries, Ann Anderson, and Chet Hendrickson

Planning Extreme Programming, Kent Beck and Martin Fowler

Extreme
Programming
Explored

William C. Wake

ADDISON–WESLEY

Boston • San Francisco • New York • Toronto • Montreal
London • Munich • Paris • Madrid
Capetown • Sydney • Tokyo • Singapore • Mexico City

The publisher offers discounts on this book when ordered in quantity for special sales. For more information, please contact

Pearson Education Corporate Sales Division
One Lake Street
Upper Saddle River, NJ 07458
(800) 382-3419
corpsales@pearsontechgroup.com

Visit us on the Web: www.awl.com/cseng/

Library of Congress Cataloging-in-Publication Data

Wake, William C.
    Extreme programming explored / William C. Wake
        p. cm.—(XP series)
    Includes bibliographical references and index.
    ISBN 0-201-73397-8
    1. Computer software—Development. 2. eXtreme programming. I. Title. II. Series.

QA76.76.D47 W34 2001
005.1'1—dc21

                                                          2001034332

ISBN 0-201-73397-8

Text printed on recycled paper

1 2 3 4 5 6 7 8 9 10–CRS–05 04 03 02 01
First printing, July 2001

To May, Tyler, and Fiona,
with love

Contents

Foreword . . . . *ix*

Preface . . . . *xiii*

Acknowledgments . . . . *xvii*

Introduction . . . . *xix*

Part 1: Programming 1

Chapter 1 *How Do You Write a Program?* 3
> *Program incrementally and test-first.*

Chapter 2 *What Is Refactoring?* 23
> *"Refactoring: Improving the design of existing code."*—Martin Fowler

Part 2: Team Practices **45**

Chapter 3 *What Are XP's Team Practices?* 47
> *We'll explore these practices and their alternatives.*

Chapter 4 *What's It Like to Program in Pairs?* 63
> *Pair programming is exhausting but productive.*

Chapter 5 *Where's the Architecture?* 75

Architecture shows up in spikes, the metaphor, the first iteration,
and elsewhere.

Chapter 6 *What Is the System Metaphor?* 85

"The system metaphor is a story that everyone—customers, programmers,
and managers—can tell about how the system works."—Kent Beck

Part 3: Process **97**

Chapter 7 *How Do You Plan a Release?*
What Are Stories Like? 99

Write, estimate, and prioritize stories.

Chapter 8 *How Do You Plan an Iteration?* 115

Iteration planning can be thought of as a board game.

Chapter 9 *Customer, Programmer, Manager:*
What's a Typical Day? 123

Customer: Questions, tests, and steering
Programmer: Testing, coding, and refactoring
Manager: Project manager, tracker, and coach

Chapter 10 *Conclusion* 143

Bibliography 147

Index 151

Foreword

Almost 200 years ago, Meriwether Lewis and William Clark set off to explore the reaches of the Missouri and look for a northwest passage to the Pacific. Trappers and adventurers had been there before them, but Lewis and Clark had a mission. Thomas Jefferson had a vision for a country that would span a continent and trade with the Far East. He expressed this vision in a letter to Lewis, a letter that managed to convey detailed requirements while leaving the expedition the flexibility they would need while out of contact. Using the letter as their guide, the Corps of Discovery collected samples, drew maps, and wrote extensive journals. Two and a half years later, the expedition returned to St. Louis, having twice crossed the continent.

Following Lewis and Clark's success, routes to the West began to open. Settlers organized themselves into convoys of covered wagons, hiring guides to get them over the more difficult stretches. They faced the unknown daily and relied on each other for protection and strength. With the coming of the railroad, travel became easier. You no longer had to be a pioneer to get to the West; all you needed was the price of a ticket. Guides were replaced with timetables, and your journey became predictable.

Nowadays, we complain if our plane is 30 minutes late when we take the children to Disneyland. A vision is turned into a plan, which a few brave souls set out to follow. As they go, they take notes and draw maps. Based on these, a generation of guides steps forward to lead the pioneers. And as the pioneers demonstrate success, entrepreneurs step in to automate the process, making what was once an adventure into a commonplace trip.

As software developers, we're at the start of a new phase of exploration. Like the United States of Thomas Jefferson, we've got some of the territory under control, but large areas still remain to be mapped and tamed. As the world comes to depend more and more on the software we produce, and as the pace of software development ratchets up from the merely frantic to the insane, we need to discover new ways to deliver value to our customers. We have to tame the development processes, and we need to do it quickly.

Fortunately, we're making some progress. We have our *visionaries*—people who see how things *could be*—and we have explorers willing to take risks in pursuit of that vision. Kent Beck had a vision for agile software development, and he used it to inspire the C3 team at Chrysler. Armed with these ideas, the team set out to explore. As they did, they recorded their experiences—first on Ward Cunningham's WikiWikiWeb (*http://www.c2.com/cgi/wiki*) and later in two great books. With Beck's *Extreme Programming Explained*, we have our marching orders. With *Extreme Programming Installed* and *Planning Extreme Programming*, we have the maps. But it still takes courage to set out, map in hand, into the unknown. After all, the process is called *extreme*, an adjective currently used to describe sports played by people too young to know they're mortal doing things too crazy to be called sports. Clearly, there be dragons out there. What we need is a guide, someone who can help us avoid the dangers, teach us the finer points, and get us safely to where we're going. Bill Wake is that guide.

Extreme Programming Explored will take you on a journey. You'll sit in on a pair-programming session and experience first-hand the interactions that take place. You and Bill will partner to refactor some code. You'll develop a database application test-first. Together you'll plan a library system. Then you'll see what a typical day looks like for a manager and a programmer and their customer.

For me, that's what makes this book special. Whereas other books are the maps, explaining what should be done and how you get from here to there, the book you are holding takes you there. It won't necessarily be easy, and there are still plenty of wrong turns and tricky problems waiting for you, the pioneer. But after reading this book, you'll know what to expect, and you'll know that others have been there before. Pretty soon, you'll be the old hand telling scary stories to the tenderfeet arriving from the East. And you'll look around with pride as you see more and more developers settling in to this area you helped to tame.

Enjoy the journey.

Dave Thomas
The Pragmatic Programmer

Preface

Extreme Programming (XP) defines a process for developing software: it addresses the problem from early exploration through multiple deliveries.

We'll explore XP from the inside to the outside.

First, XP is a programming discipline. We'll look at a core innovation: how "test-first" changes the programming process itself. We'll also discuss *refactoring*—the way XP programmers improve their code.

Second, XP is a team discipline that has developed practices that help produce a high-performing team. We'll compare XP to alternative practices and see XP's team practices in action.

Finally, XP is a discipline for working with customers. XP has specific processes for planning and daily activity. We'll see how a team might schedule a release or iteration and what the team does all day.

Why Read This Book?

If you've heard anything about XP, you probably have had questions about the mechanics or the purposes of various aspects of XP. I've tried to capture the questions I've had, along with answers I've found.

Several things about XP were surprises to me, particularly the tight cycle of test-first programming (only a couple minutes long), the use of a metaphor, and the starkness of the division of labor between customer and programmer. We'll look at these and many other topics.

You, the reader, may have several areas of interest that bring you to this book:

 ⬦ *Java and object-oriented programming.* The first section of the book uses Java programming language examples to focus on test-first programming and refactoring. Programmers may find the discussion of team practices useful as well, particularly the ideas about metaphors and simple design.

 ⬦ *Extreme programming, from the perspectives of programmer, customer, and manager.* We'll explore several areas more deeply or from a different perspective than the rest of the XP literature, especially the team-oriented practices, the metaphor, the planning process, and daily activities.

 ⬦ *Software process in general.* XP is one of several so-called agile, lightweight, adaptive processes that have been introduced in the last few years. By taking an in-depth look at XP's process, we can more clearly delineate where XP fits in with these related processes.

Who Is the Author? Why This Book?

I'm "just a programmer," with about 15 years of experience, about half in compiler development and the rest in library, telecom, and financial services.

I attended the first XP Immersion class in December, 1999. Although I had read *Extreme Programming Explained*, and much of the XP material on the Web, I was surprised by how test-first programming really worked (a much quicker cycle than I'd expected).

The question of testing user interfaces came up in the class; Kent Beck said he didn't usually develop user interfaces test-first, but asked, "Could you?" That inspired me to write an essay on the topic.

I write to learn, so as I explored various XP topics, I wrote a series of articles I called "XPlorations" and made them available on the Web. With the encouragement of my peers, I've adapted some of those essays for this book in order to give a coherent view of the issues surrounding XP.

What Is the Philosophy of This Book?

Be concrete. Use real (or at least realistic) examples. When code appears, it is Java code.

Answer questions. Because most of the chapters originally were written as essays for myself as I learned or taught others, each chapter begins with a question and a short answer. Many chapters include a Q&A (question and answer) section as well.

Be focused. Make each chapter focus on one topic. Tie it to other chapters where possible.

Be precise but informal. I use "I," "we," and "you" a lot. For the most part, "you" is addressed to a programmer, but, in some sections, the word may be addressed to managers or customers.

Bring experiences to bear. I relate this material to real experiences.

Acknowledgments

I've always seen books with an "Acknowledgments" section listing all the people who helped the author directly or otherwise. Now I'm in the position of creating such a list, and I realize I've certainly forgotten the names of many who helped get me here. So I offer my apologies to those I've forgotten and my thanks to all.

Thanks first to Kent Beck and Dave Thomas, who have given me inspiration, encouragement, and critique, all along the way. They, as well as Ken Auer, Ward Cunningham, Martin Fowler, Jim Highsmith, Bob Martin, Frank Westphal, and others, gave me courage to start this project.

Several people gave me substantial reviews of one or more drafts of the whole manuscript: Kent Beck, Tammo Freese, Andy Hunt, Harris Kirk, William Kleb, Steve Metsker, Dave Thomas, Georg Tuparev, Steve Wake, Don Wells, and Frank Westphal. Next time I'm programming (or writing), I want one of them sitting by my shoulder.

Past and present co-workers at Capital One, for discussions and the opportunity to teach and learn: Paul Given, Bob Holstein, Harris Kirk, Michele Matthews, Steve Metsker, Tim Snyder, Steve Wake, Joe Wetzel, and others. Bob Holstein and Steve Metsker sent me to XP Immersion 1, which got me seriously started on this subject. Steve Wake has read through and critiqued more drafts than anyone, and he helped brainstorm the metaphor catalog.

People in the XP community, for conversations small and large: Ann Anderson, Tom Ayerst, Serge Beaumont, Dennis Brueni, Bill Caputo, Quenio dos Santos, Joi Ellis, Chris Fahlbusch, Ed Falis, Malte Finsterwalder, Steve Freeman, Peter Gassmann, Dan Green, Chet Hendrickson, Michael Hill, Kari Hoijarvi, Dwight Hyde, Andrey Khavryutchenko, Robert Lauritzen, Duncan McGregor, Jim Mead, Zohar Melamed, Chris Morris, Miroslav Novak, Shinichi Omura, Christian Pekeler, Rekha Raghu, Don Roberts, Gilbert Semmer, Sinan Si Alhir, Philippe Vanpeperstraete, Joseph Vlietstra, Doug Wake, Daniel Weinreb, Roger Whitney, Laurie Williams, Mark Windholtz, Torben Wölm, Diane Woods, Park Sung Woon, Tilak Yalamanchili, Fred Yankowski, Jason Che-han Yip, and others. Not everybody agreed with me on everything, of course, but I appreciate the interaction and the opportunity to learn from them.

Thanks to those who have let me borrow some of their words: Harris Kirk, Bob Koss, Steve Metsker, Ron Jeffries, Dave Thomas, and Christopher Painter-Wakefield.

At Addison-Wesley: Ross Venables, who got me started, and Mike Hendrickson and Marilyn Rash, who are bringing it in. I know there are many other people there who make a book happen; they're unknown to me, but not unappreciated.

My family: my parents, Caroline and Bill; my siblings, Becky, Lynn, Doug, and Steve; and especially May, Tyler, and Fiona, who support my "always scribbling."

William C. Wake
William.Wake@acm.org
http://www.xp123.com

Introduction

Programming, team practices, and processes.

Extreme Programming (XP) is a new, agile approach to developing software. An XP team uses an on-site customer, a particular planning approach, and constant testing to provide rapid feedback and high-bandwidth communication. This helps the team maximize the value it delivers.

Let's consider a traditional approach to software development:

> The user's (customer's) group arranges with the development group to have one or more analysts assigned to a project. Over a series of weeks and months, the analysts meet with the users for several hours a week. The analysts produce a set of documents, perhaps including things such as a Vision Statement or Use Cases. The users and the project manager, and perhaps the programming team as well, review these documents and negotiate a release.
>
> The programmers take the specifications, and several months later they produce a system that more or less does

what it was intended to do. It's often a close call at the end, as people find out what they missed and realize what's changed since the documents were written. In the end, the customer does a user acceptance test, and then the system is released.

Often the whole process takes longer than anybody expects, several features are missing, the quality is not what the users want it to be, and the documents are no longer up to date.

Some teams are more iterative:

During development, the team builds a full version of the system, perhaps every 6 to 8 weeks. In the best case, analysis and development proceed in parallel, supporting each other.

An XP approach emphasizes customer involvement and testing:

The customer contacts an XP development group to start a project. The team members ask that the customer sit with them during development.

Early on, the team focuses on exploration and release planning; the customer writes stories, the programmers estimate them, and the customer chooses the order in which stories will be developed.

Later, there is more emphasis on production code. The team works iteratively: the customer writes tests and answers questions while the programmers program.

The XP customer has frequent opportunities to change the team's direction if circumstances change: iterations provide runnable software every two weeks. Because testing is so prominent, the customer is aware of the project's true status much earlier.

In XP, there is a clear separation between the roles of the customer and the programmer. They are on the same team, but they have different decisions to make. The customer owns "what you get," and the programmer owns "what it costs." This becomes apparent when you see who gets to make which decisions.[1]

The customer decides:

- ✦ *Scope:* What the system must do

- ✦ *Priority:* What is most important

- ✦ *Composition of releases:* What must be in a release for it to be useful

- ✦ *Dates of releases:* When the release is needed

The Programmers decide:

- ✦ *Estimated time:* How long it will take to add a feature

- ✦ *Technical consequences:* Programmers explain the consequences of technical choices, but the customer makes the decision

- ✦ *Process:* How the team will work

- ✦ *Detailed schedule:* When parts will be completed within an iteration

The issue of technical consequences comes up because the customer must live with the result. For example, an object-oriented database might let the team work faster, but the customer might prefer a relational database for one or more reasons such as risk management and minimizing disruption of the support process. The developers might be 100 percent right: "Yes, it would be faster to develop that way," but development time is not the customer's only consideration.

The practices of XP help enforce the split between customer and programmer responsibilities. This division of labor helps keep the

---

1. This list is summarized from Beck. 2000. *Extreme Programming Explained,* p. 55.

whole team on track by making the decision consequences visible. For example, if a customer wants the software to generate a new report this week, the XP team is happy to provide it. They'll report the technical risk (if any) and estimate what it will cost. Then the customer gets to pick what will be dropped to allow time for development.

What happens if there's a conflict? What if the customer wants certain features by a particular date, but the programmers estimate that it will take longer than that? XP provides several options: the customer can accept less scope, the customer can accept a later date, the customer can spend time or money exploring an alternative, or the customer can find a different programming team. What XP doesn't let you do is say, "Let's try anyway—we'll catch up later."

XP Is an Onion

You can think of XP as an onion (Figure I.1). The innermost layer is programming. XP uses a particular programming style, usable even by a solo developer. (But as we'll see later, XP discourages solo development.) The middle layer consists of a set of team-oriented practices. The outer layer defines the process by which a programming team interacts with its customer.

This book reflects the layered approach, with sections corresponding to the three layers. Each chapter answers questions pertinent to its layer, reflecting questions I've had to answer in learning XP.

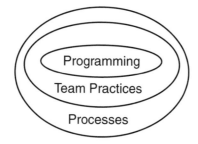

FIGURE I.1 XP Is an Onion

XP as "The 12 Practices"

Another (related) way to look at XP is as a set of practices. In *Extreme Programming Explained*, Kent Beck lays out a set of 12 core practices that serve as a starting point for an XP team. I'll map those practices to the layers as follows:

- *Programming:* Simple design, testing, refactoring, coding standards

- *Team practices:* Collective ownership, continuous integration, metaphor, coding standards, 40-hour week, pair programming, small releases

- *Processes:* On-site customer, testing, small releases, planning game

Notice that there's some overlap because a few practices cross categories.

Part 1: XP as Programming

XP programmers write code using incremental test-first programming: unit-test a little at a time, then code just enough to make the test work. There is always a test to justify any new code. In Chapter 1, we'll develop the core of a library search system using this approach.

A program isn't completed just because it happens to work. XP strives to keep the whole system as flexible as possible by keeping it as simple as possible. Refactoring improves the code while ensuring it still passes all its tests. Simpler code can live longer. In Chapter 2, we'll refactor a Java program that generates a Web page. By cleaning up obvious problems, we prepare the code for radical design changes.

Part 2: XP as Team Practices

Chapter 3 looks at the team-oriented practices and some alternatives to them: code ownership, integration, overtime, workspace, release schedule, and coding standard.

Pair programming provides on-the-spot design and code reviews for each line of production code. Many teams struggle to introduce it, but XP regards pairing as a key mechanism for ensuring quality and team learning. Chapter 4 looks at a dialogue in which two programmers pair on a tricky problem.

XP doesn't emphasize "architecture" as a driving mechanism, but XP programs do have an architecture. The metaphor, the design, and the development process support an XP program's architecture (Chapter 5).

The metaphor provides a conceptual framework and shared vocabulary for a system. Part 2 ends with Chapter 6, which explores how metaphors can drive the conceptualization and realization of a couple of different types of systems.

Part 3: XP as Processes

XP uses the notion of a planning game for planning the release (weeks to months) and for planning iterations (one to three weeks). The planning game uses two types of player—Customer and Programmer—and defines which player can make which move. In this way the process maintains a critical division of labor: Customer determines value, Programmer determines cost.

Chapter 7 describes release planning. In the *release planning game*, the goal is to define the set of features required for the next release. Release planning centers on user stories. The customer-writes the stories, the programmers estimate the stories, and the customer plans the overall release. We discuss the release planning process and give examples of stories a customer might write.

Chapter 8 demonstrates the *iteration planning game,* which is similar to the release planning game but focuses on a time scale of weeks rather than months. The customer chooses the stories for the iteration, and the programmers estimate and accept the corresponding tasks. We describe this process as a board game.

Chapter 9 describes the activities of the customer, programmer, and manager during the day-to-day work of an iteration.

XP Resources

For more information, see the references at the end of each chapter and the bibliography at the end of this book. The code examples and other supporting materials are available online at *http://www.xp123.com*.

Part 1

Programming

Chapter 1

How Do You Write a Program?

Program incrementally and test-first.

Program incrementally, because we program in a tight cycle: not even a whole class at a time, but rather a few lines of code or a method at a time.

Test-first, because we write automated, repeatable unit tests before writing the code that makes them run.

This approach yields several benefits:

✧ *The code is testable:* It was built to be so.

✧ *The tests are tested:* We saw the tests fail when the code to support them wasn't there, and saw them pass when the code was added.

✧ *The tests are repeatable:* They are captured as code.

✧ *The tests help document the code:* Anybody who needs to see how the object works, or needs to make changes, can see and run the tests.

* *The design is minimal:* We get "just enough design" to support the tests we've written.

To demonstrate the approach, we will develop a small bibliographic system, test-first. We will see how unit tests and simple design work together. The coding process occurs in small steps, with just enough new code to make each test run. There's a rhythm, like a pendulum in a clock: test a little, code a little, test a little, code a little.

Unit Tests and JUnit

Unit tests are the key to test-first programming. We'll use the JUnit framework (for Java), developed by Kent Beck and Erich Gamma, and available from *www.junit.org*. Test frameworks for several other languages are available at *http://www.xprogramming.com*.

The following is the typical pattern for a unit test:

* Set up a few objects.

* Call some methods that affect those objects.

* Make some assertions about the resulting state.

With JUnit, we put our tests in a stereotypical class. The following is an example with a test about a couple of methods of Vector:

```
import junit.framework.*;
public class TestVector extends TestCase {
    public TestVector(String name) {super(name);}

    protected void setUp() {
        // stuff to do before each test case
    }

    public void testAddElement() {
        // setup
        Vector v = new Vector();

        // call methods
```

```
        v.addElement("Some string");
        v.addElement("Another string");

            // asserts
        assertEquals(2, v.size());
    }

    public void testSomethingElse() {
        // another test
    }
}
```

A TestRunner class will run this test by calling setUp(), then a method starting test; it will call setUp() again, then the other test method. (Individual tests may be run in any order.) If any test fails its assertion, the error is logged.

JUnit has several other features; see its documentation for more information.

Design

Suppose that we have bibliographic data with author, title, and year of publication. Our goal is to write a system that can search that information for values we specify. We have in mind an interface like the example shown in Figure 1.1.

We'll divide our work into two parts: the model and the user interface. This chapter demonstrates test-first programming in development of the model. For a quick note on how the test-first approach can be applied to user interfaces, see the sidebar at the end of this chapter.

We'll begin with a brief design session. Initially, we know we have a collection of Documents. Documents know their attributes (author, title, and year).

A Searcher knows how to find Documents: given a Query, it will return a Result (the set of matching Documents), as shown in Figure 1.2.

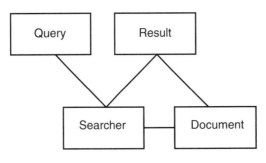

FIGURE 1.1 User Interface for a Search System

FIGURE 1.2 Four Key Objects

Notice that our design fits onto a handful of cards. As we'll discuss in the chapter on metaphors, our design uses the "naive metaphor": objects are based on domain objects.

Following this design, we'll create our unit tests (and our classes) bottom-up: Document, Result, Query, and Searcher. ("Bottom-up" isn't required by test-first; it just looks easy in this case.)

Document

A Document needs to know its author, title, and year. We'll begin by creating a "data bag" class, beginning with its test.

```
public void testDocument() {
    Document d = new Document("a", "t", "y");
    assertEquals("a", d.getAuthor());
    assertEquals("t", d.getTitle());
    assertEquals("y", d.getYear());
}
```

We haven't created the Document class yet; therefore, this test doesn't compile; so we create the class with stubbed-out methods.

Run the test again to make sure it fails. This may seem funny—don't we want the tests to pass? Yes, we do. But by seeing a test fail first, we get some assurance that the test is valid. And once in a while, a test passes unexpectedly: "that's interesting!"

Finally, fill in the constructor and the methods to make the test pass.

This mini-process is highlighted in Figure 1.3. (We'll look at refactoring in the next chapter.)

This process ensures that you've seen the test both fail and pass, which gives you assurance that the test did test something, that your change made a difference, and that you've added valuable functionality.

Kent Beck and others will tell you not to bother writing tests for simple setters, getters, and constructors: you only need to "test everything that could possibly break" (and those that can't break). Kent says, "Write too many tests, then back off."

I've used setter and getter tests in this example, but my own style is moving away from them. I just try to be aware that a large number

The Test/Code Cycle in XP

✧ Write one test.

✧ *Compile the test.* It should fail to compile, because you haven't yet implemented the code that the test calls.

✧ Implement just enough to compile. (Refactor first if necessary.)

✧ *Run the test and see it fail.*

✧ Implement just enough to make the test pass.

✧ *Run the test and see it pass.*

✧ Refactor for clarity and to remove duplication.

✧ Repeat from the top.

FIGURE 1.3 XP's Test/Code Cycle

of setters and getters is a sign that the class may not be pulling its weight, and there may be a better redistribution of class responsibilities.

How long does this cycle take? From one to five minutes, maybe ten at the outside.

What if it's taking longer? Move to smaller tests.

Really—five minutes? Yes.

Isn't this bouncing around between test and code kind of high overhead? Not really. For example, in IBM's VisualAge for Java, you write the test and click "Save." The environment signals a compiler error, so you write the stub and "Save." Then you click the "Run" button of JUnit (which just stays running); this reloads the new classes and runs the tests again, which show red. Then write the real code, "save," and run the tests one last time for a green bar.

If you were planning to write unit tests anyway, all you've added is the burden of writing a failing stub and running the tests an extra time to see them fail. Even if you're working from a command line, it's not that bad, because you can keep windows open for compilers and so on.

Won't all this test code slow you down later during maintenance? If things change, you have to update tests as well as code. No, the tests actually speed you up in maintenance, because they give you the confidence to change things, knowing that a test will warn you if you've done something wrong. If interfaces change, you do have to change tests as well, but that's not really that hard. Furthermore, you may find that test-first programming tends to drive you toward a more stable design in the first place.

Result

A Result needs to know two things: the total number of items and the list of Documents it contains. First we'll test that an empty result has no items.

```
public void testEmptyResult() {
    Result r = new Result();
    assertEquals(0, r.getCount());
}
```

Create the Result class and stub out its `getCount()` method. See it fail until you add `return 0;` as its implementation. Notice how we've put the simplest possible solution in place.

Next test a result with two documents.

```
public void testResultWithTwoDocuments() {
    Document d1 = new Document("a1", "t1", "y1");
    Document d2 = new Document("a2", "t2", "y2");
    Result r = new Result(new Document[]{d1, d2});
    assertEquals(2, r.getCount());
    assertSame(d1, r.getItem(0));
    assertSame(d2, r.getItem(1));
}
```

Add the `getItem()` method (returning null) and watch the test fail. (I'm going to stop mentioning that, but keep doing it. It takes a few seconds, but it gives you that extra bit of reassurance that your test is valid.) Implementing a simple version of Result will give the following:

```
public class Result {
    Document[] collection = new Document[0];

    public Result() {}

    public Result(Document[] collection) {
        this.collection = collection;
    }

    public int getCount() {return collection.length;}

    public Document getItem(int i) {return collection[i];}

}
```

The test runs, so we're done with this class.

Notice how we've taken a simple approach to representing the set of documents: an array. This is an example of the XP principle "Do The Simplest Thing That Could Possibly Work" (sometimes abbreviated DTSTTCPW). The current system doesn't require anything fancier than arrays. We "know" the day will come when it requires more, and we will address it when it does.

Is that really how you do it, or are you simplifying it for the example? That's really how I do it. The hardest part to convey is that even in writing production code, I rarely write more than a few lines of code (usually fewer than five) without writing another test.

Query

We can represent the Query as just its query string, which contains the words we're searching for, as follows:

```
public void testSimpleQuery() {
    Query q = new Query("test");
    assertEquals("test", q.getValue());
}
```

Create the Query class with a constructor, so that it remembers its query string and reports it via `getValue()`.

Searcher

The Searcher is the most interesting class. The easy case is first: we should get nothing back from an empty collection of Documents.

```
public void testEmptyCollection() {
    Searcher searcher = new Searcher();
    Result r = searcher.find(new Query("any"));
    assertEquals(0, r.getCount());
}
```

This test doesn't compile, so stub out the Searcher class.

```
public class Searcher {
    public Searcher() {}
    Result find(Query q) {return null;}
}
```

The test compiles, but fails to run correctly (because `find()` returns null). We can fix this with the change: `public Result find(Query q) {return new Result();}`.

Things get more interesting when we try real searches. Then we face the issue of where the Searcher gets its documents. We'll begin by passing an array of Documents to the Searcher's constructor. But first, a test.

```
public void testOneElementCollection() {
    Document d = new Document("a", "a word here", "y");
    Searcher searcher = new Searcher(new Document[]{d});
    Query q1 = new Query("word");
```

```
        Result r1 = searcher.find(q1);
        assertEquals(1, r1.getCount());

        Query q2 = new Query("notThere");
        Result r2 = searcher.find(q2);
        assertEquals(0, r2.getCount());
}
```

This test shows that we have to find what *is* there and not find
what's *not* there.

To implement this, we have to provide the new constructor that
makes the test compile (though it still fails). Then we have to get
serious about implementation.

First, we can see that a search must retain knowledge of its collection between calls to find(), so we'll add a member variable to keep
track and have the constructor remember its argument, as follows:

```
Document[] collection = new Document[0];

public Searcher(Document[] docs) {
    this.collection = docs;
}
```

Now, the simplest version of find() can iterate through its documents, adding each one that matches the query to a Result, as follows:

```
public Result find(Query q) {
    Result result = new Result();
    for (int i = 0; i < collection.count; i++) {
        if (collection[i].matches(q)) {
            result.add(collection[i]);
        }
    }
    return result;
}
```

This looks good, except for two problems: Document has no
matches() method, and Result has no add() method.

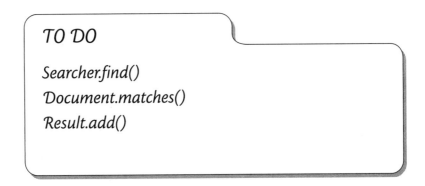

TO DO

Searcher.find()
Document.matches()
Result.add()

FIGURE 1.4 A "To Do" List

By now, we have several things occurring. I often find it helpful to make a "To Do" card, where I capture a list of things I intend to do, as shown in Figure 1.4.

Let's add a test: we'll check that each field can be matched and that a document doesn't match queries it shouldn't.

```
public void testDocumentMatchingQuery() {
    Document d = new Document("1a", "t2t", "y3");
    assert(d.matches(new Query("1")));
    assert(d.matches(new Query("2")));
    assert(d.matches(new Query("3")));
    assert(!d.matches(new Query("4")));
}
```

There are three situations for queries that we should deal with eventually: empty queries, partial matches, and case sensitivity. For now, we'll assume empty strings and partial matches should match, and that the search is case-sensitive. In the future, we might change our mind.

This is enough information to let us implement `matches()`.

```
public boolean matches(Query q) {
    String query = q.getValue();
```

```
    return
        author.indexOf(query) != -1
    || title.indexOf(query) != -1
    || year.indexOf(query) != -1;
}
```

This will enable `testDocumentMatchingQuery()` to work, but `testOneElementCollection()` will fail, because Result has no `add()` method yet. So we'll add a test for the method `Result.add()`:

```
public void testAddingToResult() {
    Document d1 = new Document("a1", "t1", "y1");
    Document d2 = new Document("a2", "t2", "y2");

    Result r = new Result();
    r.add(d1);
    r.add(d2);

    assertEquals(2, r.getCount());
    assertSame(d1, r.getItem(0));
    assertSame(d2, r.getItem(1));
}
```

This test fails; we need to implement the `add()` method. But first, some refactoring of the existing code is needed. Result remembers its Documents in an array, but that is not the best choice for a structure that needs to change its size. We'll change to use a Vector.

```
Vector collection = new Vector();

public Result(Document[] docs) {
    for (int i = 0; i < docs.length; i++) {
        this.collection.addElement(docs[i]);
    }
}

public int getCount() {return collection.size();}

public Document getItem(int i) {
    return (Document)collection.elementAt(i);
}
```

- -

Make sure that the old unit tests `testEmptyResult()` and `test ResultWithTwoDocuments()` still pass. Add the following new method:

```
public void add(Document d) {
    collection.addElement(d);
}
```

Let's consider the `Result(Document[])` constructor. It was introduced to support the `testResultWithTwoDocuments()` test, because it was the only way to create Results containing documents. Later, we introduced `Result.add()`, which is what the Searcher needs. The array constructor is no longer needed. So we'll put on a testing hat and revise that test. Instead of

```
Result r = new Result(new Document[]{d1,d2});
```

we'll use

```
Result r = new Result();
r.add(d1);
r.add(d2);
```

We verify that all tests still pass, so it is now safe to remove the array-based constructor. We run the tests again to make sure nothing else used that constructor. We also see that `testAddingToResult()` is now essentially a duplicate of `testResultWithTwoDocuments()`, so we'll remove the latter. It's not unusual for tests to change somewhat during refactoring; the class interface may change, or the goals of a test may change.

At last, all our tests pass for Document, Result, Query, and Searcher.

Loading Documents

Where does a Searcher get its Documents? Currently, you call its constructor from the main routine, passing in an array of Documents. Instead, we'd like the Searcher to own the process of loading its Documents.

We begin with a test. We pass in a Reader, and are prepared to see exceptions. We've also postulated a `getCount()` method, used by the tests to verify that something was loaded. An advantage of having the tests in the same package as the class under test is that you can provide nonpublic methods that let tests view an object's internal state. (Most of the time we don't need this: we can almost always test an object adequately via its public interface.)

```
public void testLoadingSearcher() {
    try {
                        // \t=field, \n=row
        String docs = "a1\tt1\ty1\na2\tt2\ty2";
        StringReader reader = new StringReader(docs);
        Searcher searcher = new Searcher();
        searcher.load(reader);
        assertEquals(2, searcher.getCount());
    } catch (IOException e) {
        fail ("Loading exception: " + e);
    }
}
```

Notice that Searcher still uses an array (the simplest choice at the time). We'll do as we did for Result: refactor to convert the array to a Vector.

```
package search;
import java.util.*;

public class Searcher {
    Vector collection = new Vector();
    public Searcher() {}

    public Searcher(Document[] docs) {
        for (int i = 0; i < docs.length; i++) {
            collection.addElement(docs[i]);
        }
    }

    public Query makeQuery(String s) {
        return new Query(s);
    }

    public Result find(Query q) {
        Result result = new Result();
        for (int i = 0; i < collection.size(); i++) {
            Document doc = (Document)collection.elementAt(i);
```

```
        if (doc.matches(q)) {
            result.add(doc);
        }
    }
    return result;
}
}
```

After verifying that the old tests pass, we're positioned to do the loading.

```
// Searcher:
public void load(Reader reader) throws IOException {
    BufferedReader in = new BufferedReader(reader);
    try {
        String line = in.readLine();
        while (line != null) {
            collection.addElement(new Document(line));
            line = in.readLine();
        }
    } finally {
        try {in.close();} catch (Exception ignored) {}
    }
}

int getCount() {
    return collection.size();
}

// Document:
public Document(String line) {
    StringTokenizer tokens = new StringTokenizer(line, "\t");
    author = tokens.nextToken();
    title = tokens.nextToken();
    year = tokens.nextToken();
}
```

Searcher's array-based constructor is no longer needed. We'll adjust the test and delete the constructor:

```
public void testOneElementCollection() {
    Searcher searcher = new Searcher();
    try {
        StringReader reader = new StringReader(
                                "a\ta word here\ty");
        searcher.load(reader);
    } catch (Exception ex) {
        fail ("Couldn't load Searcher: " + ex);
    }

    Query q1 = searcher.makeQuery("word");
    Result r1 = searcher.find(q1);
    assertEquals(1, r1.getCount());

    Query q2 = searcher.makeQuery("notThere");
    Result r2 = searcher.find(q2);
    assertEquals(0, r2.getCount());
}
```

Looking Back

Put on a design hat, and look at the methods we've developed from two perspectives: the search client and the Searcher class (Table 1.1). Who uses each public method?

Looking at the Document and Query classes, I wonder if they are doing enough (each being not much more than a "data bag"). But both seem like good, meaningful "near-domain" classes, so we'll

TABLE 1.1 Public Methods

Search client	Searcher class
Document.getAuthor()	new Document()
Document.getTitle()	Document.matches()
Document.getYear()	Query.getValue()
new Query()	new Result()
Result.getCount()	Result.add()
Result.getItem()	
Searcher.find()	

hold off on any impulse to change them. The Result and Searcher classes feel like they have the right balance.

Q&A

Doesn't this development process generate a lot of blind alleys? For example, we changed data structures from arrays to Vectors (twice!). Is this a flaw in our process? No, it's not a flaw. The array was an adequate structure when it was introduced, and it was changed when necessary. We don't mind simple solutions, as long as they're never one-way dead ends. We are not omniscient, so there will be times we need to change our minds; the key is making sure we never get stuck with a bad or overly complex design.

How many tests should we expect to have? Don't be surprised if your unit test code is one to three times as big as the code under test.

Summary

We've developed the bibliographic system's model in typical XP style, emphasizing simple design and a process of alternately testing and coding. The unit tests supported us in designing, coding, and refactoring. The resulting system could have either a simple command line or a graphical user interface attached to it.

Resources

Beck, Kent. 2000. *Extreme Programming Explained*. Boston: Addison-Wesley.

Fowler, Martin, Kent Beck, John Brant, William Opdyke, and Don Roberts. 1999. *Refactoring: Improving the Design of Existing Code*. Reading, MA: Addison-Wesley.

JUnit. Available from *http://www.junit.org*. INTERNET

Wake, William C. 2000. "A Java Perspective." In *Extreme Programming Installed,* by Ron Jeffries, Ann Anderson, and Chet Hendrickson. Boston: Addison-Wesley.

A sequel to this chapter.

- -

Chapter 2

What Is Refactoring?

"Refactoring: Improving the design of existing code."
—Martin Fowler

Refactoring is the process of improving the design of code without affecting its external behavior. We refactor so that our code is kept as simple as possible, ready for any change that comes along.

See Martin Fowler's book *Refactoring* (1999) for a full discussion of the subject.

In this chapter, we'll start with some realistic code and work our way through several refactorings. Our code will become more clear, better designed, and of higher quality.

What do we need for refactoring?

- ✧ Our original code

- ✧ Unit tests (to ensure we haven't unwittingly changed the code's external behavior)

- ✧ A way to identify things to improve

- ✧ A set of refactorings we know how to apply
- ✧ A process to guide us

Original Code

The following code was designed to generate a Web page, by substituting strings for %CODE% and %ALTCODE% in a template read from a file. The code works, but a performance test showed that it is too slow; the prime reason is that it creates too many temporary strings. Once our attention is called to it, we see that this code needs a good cleanup as well.

```java
import java.io.*;
import java.util.*;

/** Replace %CODE% with requested id, and
**   replace %ALTCODE% w/"dashed" version of id.
*/
public class CodeReplacer {
    public final String TEMPLATE_DIR = "templatedir";
    String sourceTemplate;
    String code;
    String altcode;

  /**
   * @param reqId java.lang.String
   * @param oStream java.io.OutputStream
   * @exception java.io.IOException The exception description.
   */
  public void substitute(String reqId, PrintWriter out)
                                 throws IOException
  {
        // Read in the template file
    String templateDir = System.getProperty(TEMPLATE_DIR, "");
    StringBuffer sb = new StringBuffer("");
    try {
      FileReader fr = new FileReader(templateDir +
                                "template.html");
      BufferedReader br = new BufferedReader(fr);
```

```java
    String line;
    while(((line=br.readLine())!="") && line!=null)
        sb = new StringBuffer(sb + line + "\n");
    br.close();
    fr.close();
} catch (Exception e) {
}
sourceTemplate = new String(sb);

try {
    String template = new String(sourceTemplate);
        // Substitute for %CODE%
    int templateSplitBegin = template.indexOf("%CODE%");
    int templateSplitEnd = templateSplitBegin + 6;
    String templatePartOne = new String(
            template.substring(0, templateSplitBegin));

    String templatePartTwo = new String(
            template.substring(templateSplitEnd,
                            template.length()));
    code = new String(reqId);
    template = new String(
        templatePartOne+code+templatePartTwo);

        // Substitute for %ALTCODE%
    templateSplitBegin = template.indexOf("%ALTCODE%");
    templateSplitEnd = templateSplitBegin + 9;
    templatePartOne = new String(
            template.substring(0, templateSplitBegin));
    templatePartTwo = new String(
            template.substring(templateSplitEnd,
                            template.length()));
    altcode = code.substring(0,5) + "-" +
                    code.substring(5,8);
    out.print(templatePartOne+altcode+templatePartTwo);
} catch (Exception e) {
    System.out.println("Error in substitute()");
}
    out.flush();
    out.close();
  }
}
```

Unit Tests

The first step in refactoring is to create unit tests that verify the basic functionality. If you're doing Extreme Programming (XP) with incremental, test-first programming, those tests exist already as a by-product of that process.

The following test requires a file named `template.html` that contains the text "xxx%CODE%yyy%ALTCODE%zzz".

```java
import java.io.*;
import junit.framework.*;

public class CodeReplacerTest extends TestCase {
  CodeReplacer replacer;

  public CodeReplacerTest(String testName){super(testName);}

  protected void setUp() {replacer = new CodeReplacer();}

  public void testTemplateLoadedProperly() {
    try {
      replacer.substitute("ignored",
                  new PrintWriter(new StringWriter()));
    } catch (Exception ex) {
      fail("No exception expected, but saw:" + ex);
    }

    assertEquals("xxx%CODE%yyy%ALTCODE%zzz\n",
                replacer.sourceTemplate);
  }

  public void testSubstitution() {
    StringWriter stringOut = new StringWriter();
    PrintWriter testOut = new PrintWriter (stringOut);
    String trackingId = "01234567";

    try {
      replacer.substitute(trackingId, testOut);
    } catch (IOException ex) {
      fail ("testSubstitution exception - " + ex);
    }
```

```
    assertEquals("xxx01234567yyy01234-567zzz\n",
                 stringOut.toString());
  }
}
```

This code uses the JUnit unit-testing framework introduced in the previous chapter.

Code Smells

Martin Fowler and Kent Beck use the metaphor of "code smells" to describe what you sense when you look at code. Code smells tend to be a "bad sign," rather than an indication that something is necessarily wrong. You may have heard a similar idea described as "anti-patterns" (after Brown et al. 1988) or "Spidey-sense" (after Stan Lee's Spider-man, 1996).

What potential danger signs might you see in code?

- Classes that are too long

- Methods that are too long

- Switch statements (instead of polymorphism)

- "Struct" classes (getters and setters but not much functionality)

- Duplicate code

- Almost (but not *quite*) duplicate code

- Overdependence on primitive types (instead of introducing a more domain-specific type)

- Useless (or wrong!) comments

- Many more...

Some smells are obvious right away; you may not detect others until you're in the middle of refactoring.

Look at the original code above, and see what problems you can identify. (Don't restrict yourself to this list!)

A Catalog of Refactorings

About half of Martin Fowler's *Refactoring* book is devoted to a catalog of refactorings. Each of these is a relatively simple transformation; Fowler explains the mechanics of the change and provides examples (Figure 2.1). For another example, not in Fowler's book, see Figure 2.2.

Extract Method	
Before	After

`// Assume all are instance`
`// variables`
 	
`void f() {`
`    ...`
`    // Compute score`
`    score = a * b + c;`
`    score -= discount;`
`}`
	`void f() {`
	`    ...`
	`    computeScore();`
	`}`
	
	`void computeScore() {`
	`    score = a * b + c;`
	`    score -= discount;`
	`}`

FIGURE 2.1 Sample Refactoring
Source: Fowler, Martin. 1999. *Refactoring: Improving the Design of Existing Code.* Reading, MA: Addison-Wesley.

Replace String with StringBuffer	
Before	After

`String a, b, c;`
`    :`
`return a + b + c;`
	`String a, b, c;`
	`    :`
	`StringBuffer sb = new`
	`    StringBuffer(a);`
	`sb.append(b);`
	`sb.append(c);`
	`return sb.toString();`

FIGURE 2.2 Sample Refactoring

This refactoring lets us replace the easy-to-read String version with a potentially more efficient StringBuffer version (or vice versa: many refactorings are appropriate to use "backward"). Some compilers can apply this particular rule for us automatically; then we can keep the readability and let the compiler do the work. For the example below, we'll apply this refactoring ourselves.

If all compilers did this reorganization automatically, would we still want this refactoring? I believe we would. The first form is shorter, but relies on the overloading of "+" in Java. The second version uses the (otherwise) uniform operator "." to handle method calls. If we ever wanted to replace the data type (using something other than String/StringBuffer), we'd be better off starting from the StringBuffer version.

Process

Work in an environment that lets you alternate testing and changing your code.

Apply one refactoring, then run the unit tests. Repeat this process until your code expresses its intent clearly, simply, and without duplication. At first, it may feel awkward to run the tests so often, but it will speed you up to do so. (It takes a few seconds to run the tests, but it reassures you that several minutes worth of changes are OK.)

When are we done? When the code

1. Passes its tests (works)

2. Communicates everything it needs to communicate

3. Has no duplication

4. Has as few classes and methods as possible

These goals are in priority order: if duplication is required to communicate, the code is duplicated. The goals are often compressed to the phrase "once and only once" ("once" to work; "only once" to avoid duplication).

- -

In *The Pragmatic Programmer*, Dave Thomas and Andy Hunt (2000) discuss a similar but more general rule known as the DRY principle ("Don't Repeat Yourself"): "Every piece of knowledge must have a single, unambiguous, authoritative representation within a system."

Going to Work

When you considered the sample code, what smells did you find? Here is what I saw:

- Long class
- Long method
- Variables could be local to method
- Useless method comment
- Could we read template once, instead of each time?
- The code is tied to using the file system
- Questionable use of "!=" for string compare
- Use of StringBuffer without append
- Reallocating StringBuffer in loop
- The `close()` methods are not in `catch` or `finally` clause
- Inconsistent/unclear exception handling
- Lots of string addition
- Almost-duplicate code in handling "%CODE%" and "%ALTCODE%"
- Lots of extraneous `new String()`s
- Magic numbers (6 and 9) and symbols
- Lots of temporary variables

The worst smell is that long `substitute()` method, so use *Extract Method* to break it up. Many of the refactorings we use are available online in the catalog at *http://www.refactoring.com.*

First, pull out `readTemplate()` as a new method:

```
String readTemplate() {
  String templateDir = System.getProperty(TEMPLATE_DIR, "");
  StringBuffer sb = new StringBuffer("");
  try {
    FileReader fr=new FileReader(templateDir+"template.html");
    BufferedReader br = new BufferedReader(fr);
    String line;
    while(((line=br.readLine())!="")&&line!=null)
      sb = new StringBuffer(sb + line + "\n");
    br.close();
    fr.close();
  } catch (Exception e) {
  }
  sourceTemplate = new String(sb);
  return sourceTemplate;
}
```

Even though the change is so simple it could not possibly fail, *run the test!* (And of course, the first time I ran the test, it failed because I forgot to call my new function, highlighting the importance of the mechanics.)

Notice also that we're not immediately chopping the routine into three or four pieces all at once; we're working one step at a time. We'll develop a steady rhythm: change some code, run the test, change some code, run the test. We never go far without verifying what we've done. If we make a mistake, it must be in the last thing we did.

Let's get the template name in one place (via *Introduce Explaining Variable*), replacing `templateDir` with

```
String templateName = System.getProperty(TEMPLATE_DIR,"")
    + "template.html";
```

(*Run the test.*) Then eliminate the `fr` variable (*Inline Temp*):

```
BufferedReader br = null;
    ...
br = new BufferedReader(newFileReader(templateName));
```

(and drop `fr.close()`.) (*Run the test.*)

Now we're in a position to fix one of the bugs we noticed: the stream is not properly closed in case of errors.

```
try {
    ...
} catch (Exception ex) {
} finally {
  if (br != null) try {br.close();}
      catch (IOException ioe_ignored) {}
}
```

(*Run the test.*)

Next look at another potential problem, the `!=` string test. We verify (by looking around and asking around) that the template reader was not intended to stop at blank lines or anything like that, so this condition is meaningless.

```
String line = br.readLine();
while (line != null) {
    sb = new StringBuffer(sb + line + "\n");
    line = br.readLine();
}
```

(*Run the test.*) Martin Fowler (1999) points out that it is safer to keep bug-fixing and refactoring separate. He would create a new test case to demonstrate the bug, complete refactoring, and only then go back to fix it. In this small example, we'll just proceed with the fixed code.

Consider the assignment to `sb`. It is redundant: there's no reason to create a new StringBuffer each time, when we can just add to the one we already have. Also, we can use `append()` to eliminate the string addition (*Replace String with StringBuffer*).

```
sb.append(line);
sb.append('\n');
```

(*Run the test.*)

Instead of `sourceTemplate = new String(sb);` let's push the work of creating the string onto the StringBuffer: `sourceTemplate = sb.toString();`. (*Run the test.*)

The routine both assigns to "sourceTemplate" and returns it. Let's move the responsibility for the assignment to the caller and just `return sb.toString()` instead. Declare the return type as String. (*Reapportion Work between Caller and Callee.*) (*Run the test.*)

For exceptions, let's declare the routine as throwing `IOException` and delete the empty catch clause; the caller will have to deal with any exceptions. This causes a change (untested! hmm...) in behavior because no partial template will be returned in case of error. We'll confirm by looking and asking whether this is OK. (*Run the test.*)

Our routine now appears as follows:

```
String readTemplate() throws IOException {
    String templateName = System.getProperty(TEMPLATE_DIR, "")
                        + "template.html";
    StringBuffer sb = new StringBuffer("");
    BufferedReader br = null;
    try {
        br = new BufferedReader(new FileReader(templateName));
        String line = br.readLine();
        while (line != null) {
            sb.append(line);
            sb.append('\n');
            line = br.readLine();
        }
    } finally {
        if (br != null) try {br.close();}
                    catch (IOException ioe_ignored) {}
```

```
    }
    return sb.toString();
}
```

The next thing I don't like is that the routine decides both where to find the template and how to read it, leaving it coupled to the file system. This may be a problem in the future (if templates were to come from somewhere else), but it's also a problem now: our test has to use an external file. I'm not sure of the right approach, so we'll defer this problem.

Substitute for "%CODE%"

The routine is still too long. We also still have the near-duplicate code for substitutions.

So next we'll *Extract Method* for replacing "%CODE%".

```
String substituteForCode(String template, String reqId) {
  int templateSplitBegin = template.indexOf("%CODE%");
  int templateSplitEnd = templateSplitBegin + 6;
  String templatePartOne = new String(
    template.substring(0, templateSplitBegin));
  String templatePartTwo = new String(
     template.substring(templateSplitEnd, template.length()));
  code = new String(reqId);
  template = new String(templatePartOne+code+templatePartTwo);
  return template;
}
```

Then we'll adjust the variable declarations left in `substitute()`. (*Run the test.*)

The first thing I notice is the string "%CODE%" and the value 6 (the length of the pattern). Pull out the pattern and use it (*Replace Magic Number with Calculation*).

```
  String pattern = "%CODE%";
  int templateSplitBegin = template.indexOf(pattern);
  int templateSplitEnd = templateSplitBegin+pattern.length();
```

(*Run the test.*)

We create a lot of new Strings too: all those `new String()` constructions are redundant, because their arguments are Strings already (*Remove Redundant Constructor Calls*).

```
String templatePartOne =
    template.substring(0,templateSplitBegin);
  String templatePartTwo =
    template.substring(templateSplitEnd, template.length());
  code = reqId;
  return templatePartOne + code + templatePartTwo;
```

(*Run the test.*)

We'll eventually want to address the remaining string addition (on the return statement), but let's take care of "%ALTCODE%" first.

Substitute for "%ALTCODE%"

Let's do the same *Extract Method* and simplification for the other case, and see where we are.

```
void substituteForAltcode(String template, String code,
                          PrintWriter out) {
  String pattern = "%ALTCODE%";
  int templateSplitBegin = template.indexOf(pattern);
  int templateSplitEnd = templateSplitBegin+pattern.length();

  String templatePartOne = template.substring(
              0, templateSplitBegin);
  String templatePartTwo = template.substring(
              templateSplitEnd, template.length());
  altcode = code.substring(0,5) + "-" + code.substring(5,8);
  out.print(templatePartOne + altcode + templatePartTwo);
  }
```

This code is *so* similar to `substituteForCode()`, it's clear we should be able to unify the two routines. But there are three differences: they look for different patterns, they substitute different values, and they write to different streams. Drive them toward duplication by passing in the patterns and replacements as arguments (*Parameterize Method*).

```
void substituteForAltCode(String template, String pattern,
  String replacement, PrintWriter out) {
  int templateSplitBegin = template.indexOf(pattern);

  int templateSplitEnd = templateSplitBegin+pattern.length();

  String templatePartOne = template.substring(
        0, templateSplitBegin);

  String templatePartTwo = template.substring(
        templateSplitEnd, template.length());
  out.print(templatePartOne + replacement + templatePartTwo);
}
      ...
  altcode = reqId.substring(0,5) + "-" + reqId.substring(5,8);
    substituteForAltCode(template, "%ALTCODE%", altcode, out);
```

(*Run the test.*)

We can address the excessive string addition by using a series of `print()` calls (*Replace String Addition with Output*), and we'll pull the buffer flush up as well.

```
    out.print(templatePartOne);
    out.print(replacement);
    out.print(templatePartTwo);
    out.flush();
```

(*Run the test.*)

The big difference now is that `"%CODE%"` results in a String, and `"%ALTCODE%"` is written to a PrintWriter. These can be reconciled via the class `java.io.StringWriter`. So make `substituteForCode()` take an argument `PrintWriter out`, and create and pass in a `new PrintWriter(new StringWriter())` as its stream (*Unify String and I/O*). (*Run the test.*)

How did I know to look for a class such as StringWriter? First, I could have talked to a co-worker and found it; there's usually someone who knows the odd corners you don't. (In XP, you start with your pair partner; if your partner doesn't know, the rest of the team is in the same room.) Second, I've used enough systems to know that many have a way to let you treat strings as I/O, and vice versa. Third, I could have learned it when I read once through the core APIs when learning the language. Finally, it *is* documented and can be found when needed.

We see that the two routines are now identical: eliminate `substituteForAltcode()`, and just call `substituteForCode()` twice (*Merge Identical Routines*). (*Run the test.*)

Back to readTemplate()

We were able to verify (by asking our customer) that it would be acceptable to read the template once at startup, rather than once per call to `substitute()`. We can declare the constructor to throw IOException, and make the call to `readTemplate()` there.

```
sourceTemplate = readTemplate(
        System.getProperty(TEMPLATE_DIR, ""));
```

(*Run the test.*)

This helps eliminate some strings we would otherwise create.

At last, we can address that old thorn: direct reading of a file to load the template. The `readTemplate()` routine currently takes a directory name and constructs a file. Instead, we'll pass in a Reader and let that do the work. First pull up construction of the FileReader into the constructor (*Reapportion Work between Caller and Callee*).

```
public CodeReplacer() throws IOException {
    String templateName =
System.getProperty(TEMPLATE_DIR, "") + "template.html";
    sourceTemplate = readTemplate(
                    new FileReader(templateName));
}
```

```
public String readTemplate(Reader reader)
                    throws IOException {
   ...
}
```

(*Run the test.*)

Next introduce a constructor that takes a Reader, which the caller is responsible for forming. (They will probably use the `getProperty()` code that was there before.)

```
public CodeReplacer(Reader reader) throws IOException {
  sourceTemplate = readTemplate(reader);
}
```

(*Run the test.*)

I'll put a testing hat back on and modify my test. We can simplify `testTemplateLoadedProperly()`, because we no longer need to do a substitution to see the template just to load it. Also, instead of setting up with the file `template.html`, we'll test using a StringReader. This helps decouple our tests from the environment.

```
final static String templateContents =
                    "xxx%CODE%yyy%ALTCODE%zzz\n";
       ...
  replacer = new CodeReplacer(new StringReader(
                            templateContents));
       ...
public void testTemplateLoadedProperly() {
  assertEquals(templateContents, replacer.sourceTemplate);
}
```

(*Run the test.*)

Finally, the `close()` call in `substitute()` is a little out of place. Because the caller of the object opens the stream, we'd like the caller to be responsible for closing the stream as well. We'll modify `substitute()` and its callers (*Reapportion Work between Caller and Callee*).

(*Run the test one last time.*)

- -

Final Result

Here's the complete new version of CodeReplacer.java:

```java
import java.io.*;
import java.util.*;
/** Replace %CODE% with requested id, and %ALTCODE% w/"dashed"
version of id.*/

public class CodeReplacer {
    String sourceTemplate;

    public CodeReplacer(Reader reader) throws IOException {
        sourceTemplate = readTemplate(reader);
    }

    String readTemplate(Reader reader) throws IOException {
        BufferedReader br = new BufferedReader(reader);
        StringBuffer sb = new StringBuffer();
        try {
            String line = br.readLine();
            while (line!=null) {
                sb.append(line);
                sb.append("\n");
                line = br.readLine();
            }
        } finally {
            try {if (br != null) br.close();}
            catch (IOException ioe_ignored) {}
        }
        return sb.toString();
    }

    void substituteCode (String template, String pattern,
                         String replacement, Writer out)
                            throws IOException {
        int templateSplitBegin = template.indexOf(pattern);
        int templateSplitEnd =
            templateSplitBegin + pattern.length();
        out.write(template.substring(0, templateSplitBegin));
        out.write(replacement);
```

```
        out.write(template.substring(
                templateSplitEnd, template.length()));
        out.flush();
    }

    public void substitute(String reqId, PrintWriter out)
                    throws IOException {
        StringWriter templateOut = new StringWriter();
        substituteCode(sourceTemplate, "%CODE%",
                    reqId, templateOut);

        String altId = reqId.substring(0,5) + "-" +
                        reqId.substring(5,8);
        substituteCode(templateOut.toString(), "%ALTCODE%",
                    altId, out);
    }
}
```

Here's CodeReplacerTest.java:

```
import java.io.*;
import junit.framework.*;

public class CodeReplacerTest extends TestCase {
    final static String templateContents =
                    "xxx%CODE%yyy%ALTCODE%zzz\n";

    CodeReplacer replacer;

    public CodeReplacerTest(String testName)
    {super(testName);}

    protected void setUp() {
        try {
            replacer = new CodeReplacer(new StringReader(
                                        templateContents));
        } catch (Exception ex) {
            fail("CodeReplacer couldn't load");
        }
    }
```

```
public void testTemplateLoadedProperly() {
    assertEquals(templateContents,
                 replacer.sourceTemplate);
}

public void testSubstitution() {
    StringWriter stringOut = new StringWriter();
    PrintWriter testOut = new PrintWriter (stringOut);
    String trackingId = "01234567";

    try {
        replacer.substitute(trackingId, testOut);
        testOut.close();
    } catch (IOException ex) {
        fail ("testSubstitution exception - " + ex);
    }

    assertEquals("xxx01234567yyy01234-567zzz\n",
                 stringOut.toString());
}

}
```

Analysis

We now have a much better routine. We've fixed a few bugs and ambiguities on the way. It's clearly much easier to read, because we've squeezed out the duplicate code. We replaced string addition with cheaper operations in several places. We've isolated our templates from the file system; instead, they use Readers to load themselves. We still have some cleanup to do: the variable names could be better (e.g., sb and br); also, the way the alternate identifier is formed is not obvious.

The new code embodies three basic things:

1. How a template is represented (currently a string)

2. How substitution is made

3. What codes and values to substitute ("%CODE%" and "%ALTCODE%")

The first two items are part of how a template works; the third is the "business logic" that tells how it's used. A stand-alone Template class would address the first two points. That was not obvious from the monster routine with which we started. This shows how our sense of the code smells can change over time: I'd now argue that an overdependence on the String type keeps us working at too low a level.

Pulling the template into a separate class would allow us to address performance even more, because we would be free to change the representation of templates. The current implementation scans the template (twice) to locate the patterns that need substitution. We might be able to preprocess a template to identify the potential substitutions. We could change the interface to the substitution process to take a list or mapping of substitutions, so we could do them all in one pass.

Summary

What have we seen?

- ⬧ We can make very small, incremental improvements to the code. At each point, the latest version is better than the one before. We don't have to take the risk inherent in "Just scrap it and start over."

- ⬧ The unit tests act as a constant safety net. We never go more than a few minutes without the reassurance they provide.

- ⬧ Some improvements allow further improvements. The need for a Template class was far less obvious in the initial code.

- ⬧ Although it's possible that some refactorings may interfere with performance, they often will open up possibilities for dramatic improvements. Extracting the `readTemplate()` method allowed us to notice it was called for every substitution when it only needed to be called once; a future version of the Template class might be able to do all substitutions in one pass. These possibilities are a much bigger factor than the "extra" procedure call that *Extract Method* originally introduced.

❖ In a handful of moves (about 20), we've substantially improved our code.

Make refactoring (including testing!) a part of your normal programming practice. Sensitize yourself to code smells, and learn refactorings that can address them. It will pay off in the simplicity and flexibility your system will have.

Resources

Beck, Kent. 2000. *Extreme Programming Explained*. Boston: Addison-Wesley.

Bentley, Jon L. 1982. *Writing Efficient Programs*. Englewood Cliffs, NJ: Prentice-Hall.

Bentley, Jon L. 1988. *More Programming Pearls: Confessions of a Coder*. Reading, MA: Addison-Wesley.

Bentley, Jon L. 2000. *Programming Pearls, Second Edition*. Boston: Addison-Wesley.

Brown, William H., Raphael C. Malveau, Hays W. McCormick III, and Thomas J. Mowbray. 1988. *AntiPatterns: Refactoring Software, Architectures, and Projects in Crisis*. New York: John Wiley and Sons.

Fowler, Martin, et al. 1999. *Refactoring: Improving the Design of Existing Code*. Reading, MA: Addison-Wesley.
    A catalog of code smells and refactorings.

Fowler, Martin. 2001. Online catalog. Available from *http://www.refactoring.com*. INTERNET.

Hunt, Andrew, and David Thomas. 2000. *The Pragmatic Programmer: From Journeyman to Master*. Boston: Addison-Wesley.

JUnit. Available from *http://www.junit.org*. INTERNET.

Lee, Stan. ed. 1996. *The Ultimate Spider-Man.* New York: Boulevard (a subsidiary of The Berkeley Publishing Group).

Part 2

Team Practices

Chapter 3

What Are XP's Team Practices?

We'll explore these practices and their alternatives.

The following are "team" practices because there is no use trying to do them alone; it does little good to be the only person integrating often or the only one on the team sticking with a coding standard.

- ✧ *Code ownership:* Who can change an object that needs to change?
- ✧ *Integration:* How and when does a team ensure that everybody's code works together?
- ✧ *Overtime:* What do you do when you run out of time?
- ✧ *Workspace:* How should a team be physically arranged?
- ✧ *Release schedule:* How often should a team release its product?
- ✧ *Coding standard:* How should the code be written?

Code Ownership

When code needs to be changed, who gets to (or has to!) change it?

Nobody ("Orphan")

In some groups, nobody owns the code. For closed-source systems, maintained by a third party, "nobody" just means "nobody here." There are other programs that are untouchables: there's no source code (it was lost years ago) or the system is too brittle or too complicated to safely change.

When code isn't owned, developers will either avoid using it or treat it as a black box. That latter approach can be especially painful: the programmers must format data going in and out; they may have to mediate between two paradigms (e.g., using screen-scraping technology); they may be unable to do things you would normally expect to be possible; there may be data denormalization and coordination problems because information has to be stored both inside and outside the system.

Avoid the situation of "nobody owns it (and nobody wants to)."

Last One Who Touched It ("Tag" or "Musical Chairs") and Whoever's Newest ("Trial by Fire")

You may have systems that are reasonably stable but still a pain to maintain. In these situations, there's typically a local cultural rule that kicks in: whoever touched it last owns the next problem (which can make it frustratingly hard to escape), or perhaps the problem is given to the least powerful person (often with the instructions, "just make it work").

This model seems very common in maintenance organizations.

One Owner per Class (or Package) ("Monogamy")

The one owner per class approach is very common in new development: authors own the code they write, until somebody explicitly takes it over.

The key is that there's a definite person in charge of a section of code. If you want it changed, you negotiate with that person. The owner may even let you change it yourself, but will retain approval rights on what you do. Sometimes the ownership will go stale: the person who did one part is gone, and it's not actively changing. Then there won't be a real owner until someone needs something done and the team assigns an owner.

The benefits of this approach are that it provides a clear method for deciding who does what work, and it lets a person develop expertise in a particular area.

There are downsides, though. If the owner isn't available to make a change when needed, the team is slowed down. (Some teams mitigate this by having emergency backups.) Sometimes the owner won't agree with a proposed change, perhaps completely vetoing it. Then clients may design around it or wrap it in a way that is worse for the system overall. Another problem is that a single owner can be in trouble and hide the fact. (The code may be deeply in trouble by the time the person's lack of expertise is noticed.)

The single-owner approach can require that interfaces be frozen too early, before they're really understood, because of the need to let clients "make progress." Refactoring can be more difficult; when interfaces are public and require a lot of cooperation to change, there is political pressure not to change them (even if they need it).

Sequential Owners ("Rental Property" or "Serial Monogamy")

Some groups have a single owner for a package at any given time, but that owner will be decided on a task-by-task or iteration-by-iteration basis.

This can be good in that it gives people variety, but they may not get a chance to build sufficient expertise to be particularly effective. But at least there's an owner, so everybody knows who to contact.

The biggest problem is that the code is like rental property: the current "owners" are really "tenants"; they know the situation is temporary, so they have less incentive to worry about the long-term value of the place (provided they can get out of their lease before it gets too bad).

Ownership by Layer ("Tribalism")

Some groups organize their software into distinct layers, or even distinct applications, and have ownership at that level. Anybody in the tribe can make any change they need to—but they keep the tribe informed about what they're doing. However, nobody from another layer would dare to jump in. (You see this with user interface versus business logic versus database, or application 1 versus application 2 versus database.)

This method overcomes some flaws of "monogamy": the "bus number" is higher, there's no chance bad code will be hidden from the subteam, and so on. (The "bus number" is the number of people that, if they were hit by a bus, would cause the project to fail.) The subteams can develop a very strong esprit de corps, which further boosts their productivity.

However, interfaces *between* layers are elevated to near "golden" status, making them even harder to change. This interferes with refactoring intended to improve the overall system design.

Communication within the subteam is usually good, but it's harder to talk across layers. A change that requires convincing one person in the "one owner" model now requires "How about our subteams meet and discuss this; is everybody open next week?" This slows down the team as whole.

Collective Code Ownership ("Everybody")

In collective ownership, the whole team owns all code. Anybody can change any part they need to.

The key benefit of this approach is that it is the least obstructive to getting things done quickly. The team's ability to refactor is improved, because there are fewer published interfaces. For the right team, this can be an effective mode. (See the next section, which describes how XP tries to retain its benefits without falling victim to its risks.)

There are potential downsides as well:

- ✧ Some people take personal pride in their code, and don't want others to touch it.

- ✧ You risk the "tragedy of the commons": "everybody is responsible" can come to mean "nobody is responsible."

- ✧ This resembles "musical chairs" carried even further, perhaps aggravating the risk that nobody will be expert enough and that nobody will care for the long-term value.

- ✧ It can be hard to read and work with someone else's code. You may get a mish-mash of styles and approaches.

- ✧ People may step on each others' toes more, because they need access to the same objects.

XP Uses Collective Code Ownership

Extreme Programming (XP) recognizes the risks in collective code ownership, but uses it anyway. XP's practices attempt to mitigate these risks:

- ✧ *Personal pride:* XP doesn't really address this, other than perhaps encouraging a shift to pride at the team level.

- ✧ *"Tragedy of the commons":* Pair programming, and unit tests running at 100%, help ensure that no person can "pollute" in secrecy. The shuffling of pairs helps make all code visible to the whole team. Refactoring can clean up any trouble that does occur.

- ✧ *Not enough expertise:* Pair programming spreads knowledge through the team. The open workspace gives others a chance to speak up when one pair seems stuck or worried. Simple design can require less "deep" expertise. Finally, tests help ensure that functionality won't diverge from the requirements.

- ✧ *Reading others' code:* A coding standard helps reduce this problem, as does the shared culture that pair programming engenders.

◇ *Stepping on toes:* Continuous integration ensures that people won't go far without rejoining the main line. The tests ensure that there is no regression.

I find that people who generally support XP often have trouble accepting that collective ownership can work. If this seems to be a problem for you, check that you're integrating often enough (next section) and pairing (next chapter).

Integration

How and when does a team ensure that all the code works together?

Just before Delivery

Some groups I've worked with have typically had developers working in private areas, picking up what they need from others as they need it. Before delivery, there's an attempt to do a "code freeze" (usually a "code slush" at that point): everybody makes sure everything is checked in, and they resolve any conflicts arising from changing interfaces (especially those that obviously break the build). (This is similar to annealing in metallurgy: at first there's a lot of activity, but as the temperature is lowered, everything settles into a low-energy state.)

The big problem with this approach is that it lets people go off in drastically wrong directions, with nothing forcing them to test (or even integrate) for days or weeks. The integration process becomes a lot of work for whoever must resolve all the problems.

Daily Builds

One way forward is to go to daily builds. Every night, the system is compiled and a "smoke test" is run.

The developer's motto becomes "Don't break the build." Developers are supposed to do their own integration testing as they check in, so there should be no surprises. (The groups I've been in with this process had a project manager who actively verified that people were checking in as they finished tasks.)

Groups evolve different mechanisms to deal with the code breaking. I've heard of groups that say "Whoever breaks the build must be in by 8:00 AM each day to check the latest build (until somebody new breaks it)." One group I was in relied on peer pressure by publicizing who broke the build. Eventually the team hired a configuration manager who had a set start time each day and whose first responsibility of the day was to identify any compilation or integration problems and get the relevant programmer(s) to fix them.

Continuous Integration

Continuous integration, which XP uses, is not literally continuous, but it does occur several times per day. Each time a developer (pair) finishes a work session, they integrate what they have done. Typically, there's a single machine for the team's integration efforts, so it's serialized "first-come, first-serve."

Integration in XP is supported by tests. Developers must keep all unit tests running at 100%. To integrate, they take their code to a machine already running at 100%. After they've integrated: if the tests are still at 100%, they're done. If not, only one thing has changed: the code they introduced. They're obligated to fix the code (perhaps with help from others) or back out the changes and throw them away. They're *not* permitted to leave the integration system in a deteriorated state.

Continuous integration is possible in XP because of the "togetherness" of the group, because it's supported by tests, and because XP provides for simpler design via refactoring.

Overtime

What do you do when you run out of time?

Work Overtime

For many teams, overtime is their first response to a schedule crunch. First, the team's hours start to stretch, then the team is asked to work weekends. Some groups go so far as to have mandatory overtime.

This path can be counter-productive. The job can turn into a "death march" (in Yourdon's phrase [1999]). People find themselves performing at a lower capacity because they're too tired to think straight. Or it takes a toll on their family life, or they put in the hours physically but not mentally.

The 40-Hour Week

XP pushes a different view, saying that a 40-hour week is more appropriate (for some value of 40). XP teams realize there may be an occasional long week, but that even two weeks of overtime in a row is a sign of other problems. What does "40" mean? It doesn't mean exactly 40; for some people it will be 35, for others 45, and so on. The number 40 indicates there is a limit.

Bob Martin talks about the "eight-hour burn": the idea that you can work so hard for eight hours that you're not good for anything beyond that anyway.

XP teams want a sustainable level of productivity. If the team can't do all they promised in an iteration, they hand back stories rather than go into "overtime" mode. XP teams use the "Yesterday's Weather" Rule: estimate that the next iteration will accomplish about as many estimated day's work as this one did. (Just as yesterday's weather is a good predictor of today's, the last iteration's pace is a good predictor of this one's.) This rule helps a team find its natural productivity level. Overtime interferes with this: if a team is doing a two-week iteration, and it requires overtime to finish the tasks promised for this iteration, odds are good that it would take overtime in the next iteration as well.

My friend, Steve Metsker, says, "Professionals should be willing to spend five hours a week (outside of work) improving themselves." There are XP teams that reserve half a day per week as "play time" (where members can do things such as learn a new programming language). This uncommitted time pays off in the main work week.

In *Planning Extreme Programming* (Beck and Fowler, 2000), Kent Beck has a great story about a team that moved from thinking "We don't have enough time" to "We have too much to do." He points out that the shift is empowering: you can't do anything about time, but you *can* do something about your tasks.

Workspaces

How should a team be organized physically?

Geographically Separate (Including Telecommuting)

Geographically separate groups are based in different locations and face the communication difficulties that implies. For example, there may be differences in language (in the worst case) and differences in time zone. Even groups nominally in the same time zone can have different hours: I worked with a group in which the workers at one site tended to get in between 8:00 and 9:00 AM, and the other group around 10:00 AM to 10:30 AM. With varying lunch and departure schedules, the core hours were 10:30 to 11:30 AM and 1:30 to 4:00 PM.

Communication problems can make this approach more costly, even though it appears cheaper on the surface. ("We can hire the best people from both locations"; "We'll start another site where it's cheaper to hire.") There are travel costs as well as communication costs (including resentment from those who travel). Most groups must co-locate once in a while. I know of a group with members located on three continents; they felt that things fell apart if they didn't meet in the same room at least quarterly.

Telecommuting takes the case of separate workspaces to the extreme, breeding more communication difficulty and more isolation. If tasks can be split in a way to minimize the need for communication, telecommuting may be a welcome approach. I've known only a couple of people who have stayed with telecommuting for more than a year or so, though.

Offices (One- or Two-Person)

Offices offer the greatest level of privacy and quiet to the developer. In *Peopleware*, DeMarco and Lister (1987) reported that those with offices did the best in their "coding wars," which they attributed to the need for programmers to reach a state of "flow."

Offices are apparently the most expensive choice, because few companies seem willing to provide them for developers. (I've found a two-person office to be far more productive than a cubicle.)

Cubicles

"Cubes" seem to be the form of office least liked by developers and most liked by the managers who put them there.

Companies I've worked with seem to be making cubicles smaller: ten years ago, the standard size was 100 square feet (including for the president of the company); today (at a smaller, different company), the standard is 54 square feet (and I'm bigger than I was then!). My current cubicle doesn't allow for two people at the desk, and even if it did, the computer doesn't fit anywhere but in the corner.

Cubes also seem to get only smaller, never bigger. A friend of mine worked for a company that would have occasional "moving weekends": you'd pack up all your stuff, and return Monday to the same office, which would be six inches smaller. By gaining six inches per cube across a football-field-size room, they could add even more cubicles.

Cubes don't allow much privacy or quiet, and they interfere with communication. (I've seen wall heights anywhere from four to eight feet, but they always seem to be open on top and never have a door.)

Open Workspace

XP specifies an open workspace, usually with small private spaces around a central area. The fast machines are in the center, for pairing. XP would like the team to hit a state at which programmers can focus on their problem but still hear enough to jump in if they can help.

The same physical structure without an XP focus can degenerate into a "bullpen": everybody is stuffed into the same space, with no private space at all. You aren't on the same project or phase, so the rhythms of your communication clash with those of others. The bullpen has been the worst office type I've experienced.

Some groups starting toward XP also take smaller steps toward open workspace, by arranging for pairing machines in a spare niche or treating a wing of cubes as a public area. Beware that some places have "hot" walls: the cubicle walls are dangerous to move because they're wired for electricity.

Figure 3.1 shows a space that a team with four programmers might use. Notice that there are a couple of machines for pairing and one where integration takes place. Individual offices are shown on the bottom. Teams usually put the best "development" machines in

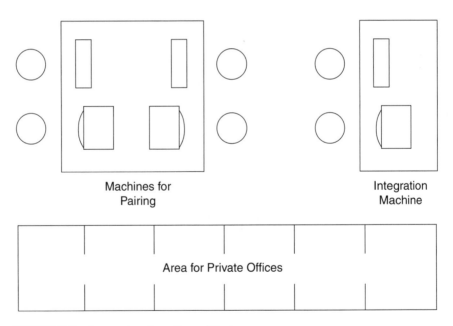

Machines for
Pairing

Integration
Machine

Area for Private Offices

FIGURE 3.1 Example of an Open Workspace

the common area and lesser machines in the offices for e-mail and Web browsing.

Release Schedule: Small Releases

How often should a team release their product? XP pushes for small but frequent releases. An XP team is trying to learn, and the more feedback they get (especially from actual use), the better. Projects that don't release for months, or even years, accumulate a lot of risk: technology will change, the business environment will change, the team will change. Small releases reduce this risk.

A release should be small, but it needs to make sense: only whole features should be included. The first release needs at least primitive versions of all major components or subsystems.

Failing to meet the goal of having small releases is the biggest mistake I've made in developing systems. When I focus on it, I find that "small" can be even smaller than I would have thought.

I've resolved to start every project with this question: "Will this interface work?" (Mimic pushing the button with your nose or forehead—see Figure 3.2.)

The answer is often "yes, if you knew these parameters." In that case we can start without a graphical user interface (GUI). If this interface isn't enough, it can get us focused on understanding what is the minimal useful system. (I've also found that it can be the developers who resist starting small; they have the vision of what the system could be and hate to back off from there.)

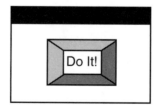

FIGURE 3.2 The Simplest Interface

In the first XP immersion class, Michael Hill described his practice of producing a Zero Feature Release (ZFR; "ziffer"). It was an end-to-end release that *did* nothing, but it established the architecture and the deployment strategy in the first iteration. It's hard to get a system into production the first time; updating it is usually a lot easier.

Coding Standard

A coding standard improves people's ability to read each other's code. In XP, it supports refactoring as well: consistently "shaped" code can be refactored more confidently.

There are several approaches to a team's coding standard:

✧ None. Ugh.

✧ Programmers choose their own style and use it everywhere. ("Then I can tell where I added code.") Ugh again.

✧ Programmers choose their own style for their own code, but use the existing style on existing code. This is the minimum I can live with. I've worked with many teams that intended to have a standard, but evolved toward this because there was no "enforcement" pressure. At least with this, you can read an individual module. This approach does interfere with refactoring: when you move code between modules, you have to reformat it as well.

✧ The team has a style and sticks to it. This is the ideal for XP. A team coding standard supports the XP practices of collective code ownership, pair programming, constant refactoring, and continuous integration.

I've seen two styles groups used in determining their standard. The first type of group has a huge battle at the beginning of the project with heated arguments over spaces and braces, but converges on a common style. The second group has no fight, but builds no group ethic either; they end up with "whatever's right for the code you're in." I'm not sure how to lead the second type along.

What coding style should be used? In a recent project where I participated in defining this (for Java), we had a six-page summary of Sun's Java coding conventions, extended with the JavaBeans naming conventions. I had created a one-page standard, but now I just try to be consistent with Sun's standard, by the mantra, "four-space indent, opening brace on the same line, JavaBeans naming conventions." I believe that a team will converge to a reasonable standard if they own code collectively, they pair, and they agree in principle to have a coding standard in the first place.

Summary

We've discussed several team practices of XP and some of the alternative choices possible.

Code ownership: Who can change an object that needs to change? XP says "collective code ownership." A non-XP team may find this to be problematic.

Integration: How and when does a team ensure that everybody's code works together? XP says "continuous integration." A non-XP team should strive toward as frequent an integration as possible.

Overtime: What do you do when you run out of time? XP says "maintain a 40-hour week." A non-XP team should strive for this as well.

Workspace: How should a team be physically arranged? XP says "open workspace." If a team is not XP, I favor offices, but with attention to the team's communication paths.

Release schedule: How often should a team release its product? XP says "small releases." If a team is not XP, I think this is still a useful target, but probably harder to hit.

Coding standard: How should the code be written? XP says "team must share a standard." If a team is not XP, I think a team standard is still appropriate.

Resources

Beck, Kent. 2000. *Extreme Programming Explained*. Boston: Addison-Wesley.

Beck, Kent, and Martin Fowler. 2000. *Planning Extreme Programming*. Boston: Addison-Wesley.

Cockburn, Alistair. 1998. *Surviving Object-Oriented Projects*, Reading, MA: Addison-Wesley.
    Discusses various models; recommends "Owner per Deliverable."

Coplien, Jim. 2001. "Code Ownership." Available from *http://www1.bell-labs.com/user/cope/Patterns/Process/section18.html*. INTERNET.

DeMarco, Tom, and Timothy Lister. 1987. *Peopleware: Productive Projects and Teams*. New York: Dorset House.

Jeffries, Ron. 2001. "Code Ownership." Available from *http://www.xprogramming.com/Practices/PracOwnership.html*. INTERNET.

Sun. 2001. "Sun's Java Coding Conventions." Available from *http://java.sun.com/docs/codeconv/index.html*. INTERNET.

Sun. 2001. "JavaBeans Conventions." Available from *http://java.sun.com/beans/docs/beans.101.pdf*. INTERNET.

Sun. 2001. "JavaDoc Conventions." Available from *http://java.sun.com/products/jdk/javadoc/writingdoccomments/*. INTERNET.

Yourdon, Edward. 1999. *Death March: The Complete Software Developer's Guide to Surviving "Mission Impossible" Projects*. Englewood Cliffs, NJ: Prentice-Hall.

Chapter 4

What's It Like to Program in Pairs?

Pair programming is exhausting but productive.

Pair programming is the practice of having two people working together to design and develop code. They are full partners, taking turns typing and watching; this provides constant design and code review. In Extreme Programming (XP), all production code is written by pairs.

Some Counter-Examples

Solo

Bob is feeling great—he got in at 6:30 AM today. He does a quick design on his next task, and starts writing tests and code. In a couple of hours, he integrates his code to the main system, and all tests pass on the first try, just as the rest of the team shows up for work that day.

Bob may be a great programmer, but as you might expect, this is not an example of pair programming. Even a team that's fully committed to pairing occasionally will face the temptation to skip it "just this once." Steve Metsker of Capital One says, "If it doesn't pinch sometimes, it's not a real methodology."

Solo programming can cause several problems. In the example, Bob may not be having as good a day as he thought; he may be passing tests, but not refactoring enough, or vice versa. The design may work, but it may not be as simple as it could be. Also, we've avoided some potential cross-team learning—Bob is the only person familiar with the code he created.

Crowd

> Janna starts her next task and asks Jay for help. Jay says, "Hey everybody—we're hooking up the joystick to the spaceship—come see!" The whole team (all ten) crowd around to watch and make suggestions. In an hour (or so), everything is working. Everybody takes a turn playing with it, and they all agree it's pretty cool.

Again, this may be good programming (and it may be fun), but it's not pair programming. The code may be fine, but it cost five times as much as it should have, and other work was delayed meanwhile. This is not to say that all pairs and all partners will always be able to handle all problems, but it ought to be rare to require the whole team for an extended time. The celebration at the end may be fine—a team needs to recognize its successes—but let's recognize it for what it is.

Disengaged

> Pat asks Ann to be her partner for the morning. Pat starts in, but Ann just sits behind her, arms and legs folded, physically present but not paying any attention. Her attitude projects, "You can make me sit here, but you can't make me help."

It takes more than physical presence to be a partner; it takes engagement in the task. In this case, if Ann is consistently a problem partner, the team will need to work to bring Ann into alignment with the team's values.

True Pairing

Don asks Lee to be his partner on the next task. Here's the card:

> ### Task: Assign Usernames
>
> Assign a unique username to each person in the system. Usernames need to be 6 to 14 characters long and must start with a letter. If it hasn't been taken already, the username should be the first initial plus the full last name.

Don and Lee talk to Carol, the customer, and find out a little more. This is a one-shot update; new entries will come with a username. Also, usernames should only have lower-case letters and digits.

Don says, "Let's start with the simplest test case: ignore the problem of duplicates, and generate 'bsmith' for 'bob smith'." He starts to write code for the test and says, "What are the parameters to substring()?" While he does the mechanics of the code, Lee looks up the method, and says, "It's one-based, like this..." and explains.

Don is focused on the typing, so Lee is free to support the task at a higher level. Instead of making a guess about the method, they've checked the real description and avoided a potential bug.

Don says, "It gets harder when we have the second 'bob smith.' We'll need to keep track of the names somehow—

we can generate them in order, I guess, and add a number field to put on the end. Let's assume they call our routine with names in order. Let me add a variable for `lastBaseName`, and then..." Lee interjects, "Wait—we need to write the test first!" Bob blushes and says, "Oh, right."

The partner can help make sure team values aren't ignored.

> Don starts again, "Hey, Carol! If you have two 'Bob Smiths' do you want the second one to be 'bsmith1' or 'bsmith2'?" Carol says, "I guess 'bsmith2', unless that's a lot harder." Don finishes the test. He makes a typo, but Lee holds off a second before pointing it out, and sure enough he fixes it before she says anything.

We see the value of an on-site customer. Again, the partner has focused on potential quality problems. Notice also the holding back; if Don had missed the typo, Lee would have spoken up, but she didn't want to interrupt his flow unnecessarily.

> Don gets the code going and the test working. Lee says, "We still need to cover the case of a name that's too short. Can I drive?" Don passes the keyboard, and she creates a test for "ye wu". After a quick consult with Carol, they decide this should be "yewu01". Lee gets the code working, and Don says, "We also have to worry about mixed case." Lee says, "Do you want to drive?"

The partner thinks strategically, making sure key cases aren't omitted. Also notice the protocol for passing the keyboard: "Can I drive?" With practice, pairs will learn when to switch.

> Lee says, "We should refactor to make all this work together cleanly." They move code around until it's clear and concise. Bob then easily drops in the new feature.
>
> Lee says, "I've been thinking. We really have three problems: the real name, the username, and the mapping between them. The real name could have many problems: case, length, and so on. Do we understand all these problems? The username has its restrictions too: length, case,

and use of digits. Finally, we need to know the mapping for each type of name. Let's sit with Carol again."

More strategic thinking, and learning as well. They've learned more about the problem structure from what they've done so far.

They snag Carol for a real sit-down. They have a good handle on the requirements for the username, but names have a lot of subtlety. Carol says, "I've been looking into it this morning, and our data is actually pretty dirty. You might see any of these (the bar separates first and last name):

- `|Mary and Bob Smith`
- `Bob|D'Santos`
- `_|John Smith`
- `Socrates|`
- `|Plato`
- `Aristotle|A. Smith`
- `|JOHN SMITH`
- `|John Smith`
- `John|Smith`
- `|'()$#"@`
- `|(none)`

and so on.

"You might see short or long names:

- `Wu|Wei`
- `Archimides|Apollonniganymedea`

and you might see some tough duplicates:

- `John|Robertsoniton`   (20 of these, followed by)
- `John|Robertsonitony`

"You'd have to be careful not to assign two 'jrobertsonitons'.

"The good news is: we're really not all that picky about what names you assign. If people really hate their username, they can call and we'll change it."

Lee asks, "What's the worst case for number of duplicates?" Carol says, "If you assume 99 or fewer, that's OK except for one crucial case: the dirty data with no alphabetic characters. There are a lot of those. You can assign them something like 'x00001' or anything, really."

This is not the best news, because they've already started working, but it's better to find out now than later.

Don and Lee go back to their code. Don says, "It looks like we're pretty far down the wrong track; should we toss this code?" Lee says, "Yup, it's the right thing to do."

The partner gives you permission to do what's needed. Sometimes, that means tossing code while retaining the learning and starting over.

They agree on a new strategy: Use a UNIX pipeline:

✧ Write out id number and the first letter of the first name concatenated to the last name.

✧ Shift the name to lowercase and delete anything not a letter.

✧ Use an "x" if the first and last name are both empty.

✧ Trim to at most 12 characters.

✧ Add enough zeros to make it at least six characters.

✧ Sort.

✧ Build and write the names. If a name duplicates the previous one, append the counter.

They set up some test cases, for example:

```
1|John|Smith
2|John|Smith
3|Wu|Wei
4||
5|(504)|555-1234
```

Don: "Can we *still* get a collision?" Lee: "I don't think so, but if we do, we'll just report an error, and do those few by hand."

They write their pipeline, trading back and forth as before. Once the tests run and they integrate, they take a well-deserved break.

Q&A

How often does the keyboard change hands? It could be every couple of minutes or a few times an hour. I would never expect to see one person type for a whole session without switching.

How often do you switch partners? I tell people to be open to switching at least every day; some will switch more often. You want cross-training, and you'll have less of it if people are joined at the hip. That said, I know some teams have introduced pairing by starting with "permanent" relationships.

Does the pair or the person own the task at hand? Typically, a person owns a task; pairs are more dynamic. A programmer might want one partner's expertise on one aspect of a task and someone else's on another.

Isn't pairing kind of hard? It can be, especially at first. In the first pair session in the XP Immersion class, we got off to a bumpy start: an extrovert with an introvert, unsure of each other's abilities, with different approaches to coding, in an unfamiliar environment, unsure what to do. We survived; it got better.

Isn't it kind of a waste to pair a senior person with a junior one? No, it's worth doing. For one thing, it can force the senior person to "think aloud"; this often exposes gaps in thinking. Furthermore, the junior person isn't passive and may ask the right question that saves an hour's or a day's work. Finally, being junior is not a permanent condition; people learn more quickly when they get to work with more experienced people.

Won't pairing cut productivity in half? Programming is not like picking strawberries; there are synergies when people work together. Pairing may have some cost, but the quality and learning make up for it. (Laurie Williams has been doing the best recent work looking at this.) Remember also that pairing builds in design and code reviews; you're not comparing raw typing speeds. For me, paired time feels most productive; the other time is tentative ("will we find everything in code review?") or wasted (yet another meeting).

Why Pair Programming Works
—Harris Kirk

The Nature of the Brain

The first reason pair programming works is that a pair can perform concurrent tactical and strategic work that reduces the overall time to complete a task. Something about the brain makes it very difficult to think at a high level at the same time you are performing a lot of activities requiring hand-eye coordination. I notice that if I try to think about why I'm typing something or what I should do next, my typing speed slows down. On the flip side, if I'm rapidly entering code or working rapidly in an IDE, the quality of my high-level thinking suffers a great deal. Pair programming creates strong synergy by filling in the other roles' weaknesses.

The second reason is potentially a quantum productivity leap and flows from the first reason. There is a great deal of design quality that only manifests when you are working rapidly. If the delay between steps is too long, I can't recall the needed information. This point is subtle but very important. Although a process may linearly reduce the time to perform a set of tasks, the quantum increases come when the speed increase allows the information to remain concurrently in memory so that the brain can suggest dramatic new designs.

The Nature of the Heart

The desire to appear competent to one's peers helps one drive toward results. In addition, new technologies are often demanding, and the availability of a partner who can share knowledge (or at least share your frustration) is very valuable. On the other hand, knowing that you have knowledge to share increases your confidence and self-esteem. Finally, there is a sense of lowered competition: when you both accomplish the same tasks, there are no feelings of being left out or anxiety that someone else just coded more in less time.

Ensuring Pair Programming Success

Reaping the benefits of pair programming requires one to confront a few inner demons. First, there is the inner critic: the constant chatterbox that relentlessly questions our abilities. For most of us, comments or questions such as "What's wrong with me, why did she see that mistake and I didn't?" are always present in our mind. Pair programming asks us to accept our fallibility and continue.

The second demon is our unwillingness both to talk and to listen. The first principle of XP is communication, and being able to communicate our needs to a programming partner requires some courage. Perhaps we need more breaks; perhaps fewer. Maybe we want to drive more. Maybe we need more silence. I've often found a need to say, "I need a moment to absorb what you just said."

Finally, pair programming requires us to be highly aware and discerning of the software, while being very respectful of our partner. Pausing before jumping in with criticisms allows you more time to understand your partner's thinking.

Pair Programming Experiences in a Nutshell

Exhausting. Four hours of pair programming feels like a full day's work. I find the XP process to be intense and exhausting. It is a major mental and psychological challenge.

Immensely satisfying. A strong feeling of accomplishment comes from knowing a task is accomplished in less time and is of higher quality than it could be if done solo. The experience is the mental equivalent of the feeling after an exercise session. Pair programming creates a synergy in that we are able to improve our interpersonal skills while delivering superior products.

Note: This sidebar was written by Kirk (July 19, 2000) for use in this book. He is currently affiliated with Capital One.

Analysis

The session above was a hard session, perhaps harder than typical. (Most sessions won't have the "restart" we saw in the middle.) We saw many interactions typical of pairs, though.

- ⬦ A partner asks for help (and receives it).

- ⬦ The partner helps with both strategic and detailed thinking.

- There's a protocol for changing hands: "Can I drive?"

- The pair learns together; cross-training is built in.

- The partner provides an ongoing quality boost: review, refactoring, unit testing, new ideas.

- The partner provides permission to do the right thing, even if it's starting over.

- If one partner forgets something, the other can remind him or her.

Pairing is a skill. It takes practice, and it doesn't start out easy for everybody. Pair programming is a crucial skill in XP, so it's worth cultivating the habit to take advantage of the benefits.

Resources

Williams, Laurie, and Robert R. Kessler. 2000. "All I Really Need to Know about Pair Programming I Learned in Kindergarten." *Communications of the ACM*, May.

Williams, Laurie, Robert R. Kessler, Ward Cunningham, and Ron Jeffries. 2000. "Strengthening the Case for Pair-Programming." *IEEE Software*, July/Aug.

Chapter 5

Where's the Architecture?

Architecture shows up in spikes, the metaphor, the first iteration, and elsewhere.

What is architecture? One IEEE definition is "the fundamental organization of a system" (IEEE 2001). In the Rational Unified Process (RUP), architecture is supported by multiple views, usually including logical view, implementation view, process view, deployment view, and use-case view. The use-case view is critical because it ties the others together. See "The 4+1 View Model of Architecture" by Philippe Kruchten (1995) for more details.

Architecture is often described as the spine or skeleton of the system, embodying the decisions that have global impact and/or would be difficult to change.

Extreme Programming (XP) places less emphasis on up-front architecture than other methods because architecture has less impact in XP: XP programmers work to keep the system flexible. XP says "embrace change," whereas architecture-driven approaches say, "Some things are hard to change, so plan the skeleton first."

On the other hand, architecture in the sense of "the essential structure" has meaning even in XP. XP addresses architecture through the following mechanisms:

◇ Spike

◇ Metaphor

◇ First iteration

◇ Small releases

◇ Refactoring

◇ Team practices

Spike

Early on, during the release planning game, the team has the opportunity to do spikes: quick throw-away (and *thrown* away!) explorations into the nature of a potential solution.

Based on the stories and the spikes, you'll decide on an approach to the system's structure. For example, suppose you have stories about managing orders over the Internet and the security that requires. You might quickly converge on a solution with a Web server, an application server, a database, and a pair of firewalls.

Another story might tell you performance constraints. To investigate performance, you might do a spike simulating many browser clients simultaneously sending queries to the system. This can help tell you how big your boxes have to be.

Another story might give you availability requirements. You'll explore replicating servers, database failover, and so on, to make sure you technically know how to manage high availability and how to help the customer assess costs and tradeoffs.

You'll also do spikes for functionality, to explore how to implement various parts of the system.

Thus the spikes you do in the exploration phase can guide you to a deployment architecture. Because the spikes begin early on, you have some lead time for ordering and installing hardware and software. Don't underestimate the value of dealing with this part early; I've seen many projects stuck in a panic as they try to get end-to-end communications all at the last minute during final installation. Addressing this early takes care of a high-risk part of many projects.

What if the customer just doesn't want *stories about performance, availability, and so on?* That's their prerogative. You have an obligation to let them know your perception of the risks, but the call is theirs to make.

What if the structure has to change later? If it has to, it has to. All you can do is give it your best analysis. With a solution in place, you'll be able to identify any problems sooner than you otherwise would, giving you more time to fix the problem.

Metaphor

During the exploration phase, and all along the way after that, you'll seek an effective *metaphor* that helps guide your solution. In literary criticism, a metaphor is a figure of speech that compares two things that aren't literally alike; in XP, the metaphor acts as a conceptual framework and provides a descriptive system of names. For example, in the online ordering system mentioned earlier, the metaphor might be centered around forms and orders.

The metaphor acts partly as the logical design in the Rational Unified Process. It identifies the key objects and their interactions. This helps orient you when you're trying to understand the functionality at the highest levels.

The metaphor may change over time as you learn more about the system and as you become inspired in your understanding of it. This is an example of the fluidity of the architecture in XP: if the conceptualization *can* be improved, it *will* be changed.

We'll look at the metaphor more in the next chapter.

First Iteration

The first iteration is key in making the system come together. From *Extreme Programming Explained* (Beck 2000):

> The first iteration must be a functioning skeleton of the system as a whole.... For the first iteration, pick a set of simple, basic stories that you expect will force you to create the whole architecture. Then narrow your horizon and implement the stories in the simplest way that can possibly work. At the end of this exercise you will have your architecture (p. 113).

Plus this:

> The first iteration puts the architecture in place. Pick stories for the first iteration that will force you to create "the whole system," even if it is in skeletal form (p. 134).

As we mentioned earlier, Michael Hill talks about using the first iteration to produce a ZFR (Zero Feature Release; "ziffer"). The team produces a system that does exactly nothing, but does it in such a way that the architecture is in place for the whole system.

The following sections describe several things you can do in the first iteration to make it easy to put the system in place.

Be Skinny

You don't need all the features of any component. For example, in a Web application, make sure the Web server, application server, database, and firewalls are all present and can talk to each other in the simplest way possible.

The book by Kernighan and Ritchie (1988) has many good features, but the one that's stayed with me the longest is the use of a "Hello, world" program: a minimal program that printed that phrase on the console.

```
int main()
{
    printf ("Hello, world!\n");
}
```

It's a small program, but notice what it takes to get it to run: obtaining access to an account, with the account set up so tools can run; running the compiler and the linker; and running the program itself. This is often the key: if you can get this program working, you can modify it as far as necessary. If you can't get even that simple program working, what chance do you have of getting a realistic program to work?

Configure Everything

Major pieces of software such as Web servers and firewalls have many ways they can be configured. By focusing the first release on an end-to-end version of the system, you help ensure that the configuration is right while your system is still simple to understand.

Establish a tricky configuration early while the system is still simple, and keep it working. This is much easier than doing it at the end, when the configuration is just as tricky but the system as a whole is more complicated too.

Shed Functionality

The focus is on an end-to-end solution. If the first iteration gets in trouble, drop any functionality you need to drop. The first iteration doesn't have to be useful; it has to be installable.

One-Button Interface

We looked at the "Do It!" interface before in Chapter 3 (see Figure 5.1).

To my regret, I've violated this approach too many times. There is always a lot of pressure to add more features "while we wait for the hardware to get here." I did a Web project that should have taken this approach, as shown in Figure 5.2.

If we'd gotten that one page working (through dozens of configuration issues), nothing else would have been very hard.

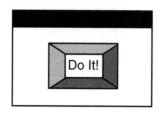

FIGURE 5.1   The Simplest Interface

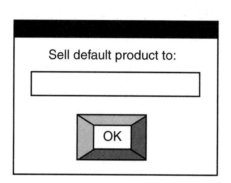

FIGURE 5.2   A Simple Sales Interface

Small Releases

XP's small releases help jell the architecture quickly. Because you're only installing at most a few months' work, you are forced to get the essential structure in place quickly. You're delivering the stories the customer values most. Because you get feedback quickly (from real use), weak areas in the architecture show up so you can correct them.

Refactoring

The spike, metaphor, and first iteration go a long way toward defining the initial architecture. Refactoring lets us manage the design going forward. Refactoring changes the design—the architecture—without changing the system's behavior; therefore, we don't risk the functionality of our program while we improve or alter its architecture.

Refactorings often work "in the small" to clean up object interfaces and interactions, but there are "big refactorings" as well. These can drastically change the form of the system. For example, Martin Fowler and Kent Beck describe refactorings such as *Separate Domain from Presentation,* which splits presentation logic from business logic.

Team Practices

There's a level at which architecture dictates things "on the ground." It's lovely to have a software architecture document that explains wonderful things about how the code should work, but it's only valuable if it reflects what people actually do.

XP forgoes the Software Architecture Document that RUP values, but still has an architecture. Pair programming (including switching pairs) helps ensure that the people know and use the approach the team is using. If a better approach is found, the team can share and learn that approach. An open workspace makes it easy to communicate. The coding standard ensures that code is written consistently

Q&A

Who defines the deployment (technical) architecture? When? The team defines the architecture. This is most evident during the exploration part of release planning. As the team understands the stories and spikes potential solutions, it learns what it needs to learn.

How is the architecture documented? As it will for all documents, the team produces enough to do the job at hand, plus whatever else the customer wants beyond that—wants badly enough to pay for. XP is light on documentation, but works hard to ensure that the team understands and communicates important information within the team.

Why produce a "skinny" version of the system? Wouldn't it be better to get, say, persistence "done right" on the first iteration, then concentrate on business logic in the next iteration, and so on? A skinny version of the system benefits both the customer and the programmers. When customers have a functioning (if minimal) system, they can define meaningful tests, they can better understand the status of development, and they can better guide development. The programmers get an opportunity to exercise all parts of the system, so they can find out early on if any part has a problem. Furthermore, by letting the needs of the slice define the needs of all layers, programmers will have less temptation to speculatively design the system's lower layers. (Remember the YAGNI rule: "You Aren't Gonna Need It.") A programmer creating, say, a persistence layer will put in everything you might need in the future; a programmer doing a slice will only do what is needed today.

If everybody *is the architect, isn't* nobody *the architect?* In a sense, that's right. In XP, the team is responsible for the architecture. Alistair Cockburn (2001) describes XP as a high-discipline process, and this is one of the places that shows up. If the team makes no effort to maintain the metaphor, doesn't bother converging to a consistent error-handling style, and doesn't focus on a functional system, it will not deliver what it needs to deliver. (The presence of a coach can help a team maintain discipline; see Chapter 9.)

So, do we want architects on the team or not? Architecture skills are still valuable, so valuable that we want the entire team cross-trained in them.

Where is the XP approach going to have trouble? I worry about two places in particular, addressed by RUP but not explicitly by XP: the process/thread structure and the data model. Threading and synchronization are hard to get right and are plagued by subtle bugs and sensitivity to change. Isolate them as much as possible, but they're still risky.

The data model is risky because it tends to be less fluid than the application code. (Consider migrating a 50-million-row table to a new structure or converting data through a process that takes days.) This may reflect my comfort level more than inherent limitations of XP, but I struggle to manage these areas through the XP philosophy.

My team isn't XP; how much of this can I use? You probably can't rely on the intense communication and oral history in XP; you'll need to document more.

Take advantage of spikes: explore to learn what your architecture needs.

Strive for a skinny implementation as your first iteration. So many problems are related to system configuration that an early iteration with minimal functionality can help explore these areas thoroughly.

Summary

Although XP doesn't focus on architecture, it has several mechanisms that ensure it is addressed:

- ✧ Spike
- ✧ Metaphor
- ✧ First iteration
- ✧ Small releases
- ✧ Refactoring
- ✧ Team practices

We talked about each of these areas and explored some questions about how they work in practice.

Resources

Beck, Kent. 2000. *Extreme Programming Explained*. Boston: Addison-Wesley.

Cockburn, Alistair. 2001. "Just in Time Methodology Construction." Available from *http://members.aol.com/humansandt/papers/jitmethy/jitmethy.htm*. INTERNET.

Fowler, Martin, Kent Beck, John Brant, William Opdyke, and Don Roberts. 1999. *Refactoring*. Reading, MA: Addison-Wesley.

IEEE. 2001. *IEEE Recommended Practice for Architectural Descriptions of Software-Intensive Systems* (IEEE std 1471). New York: IEEE.

Kernighan, Brian W., and Dennis M. Ritchie. 1988. *The C Programming Language*, Second Edition. Englewood Cliffs, NJ: Prentice-Hall.

Philippe Kruchten. 1995. "The 4+1 View Model of Architecture." *IEEE Software*, 12(6), 42–50. Available from *http://www.rational.com/products/whitepapers/350.jsp*. INTERNET

Chapter 6

What Is the System Metaphor?

"The system metaphor is a story that everyone—customers, programmers, and managers—can tell about how the system works."
—Kent Beck

Why Seek a Metaphor?

According to *Webster's Dictionary* (Allee, ed.) a metaphor is "a figure of speech that makes an *implied* comparison between things that are not *literally* alike."

In the literalistic world of software, why would we want something as fuzzy as a metaphor for a system? The following are several reasons.

Common Vision

To enable everyone to agree on how the system works. The metaphor suggests the key structure of how the problem and the solution are perceived. This can make it easier to understand what the system is, as well as what it could be.

Shared Vocabulary

The metaphor helps suggest a common system of names for objects and the relationships between them. This can become a jargon in the best sense: a powerful, specialized, shorthand vocabulary for experts. Naming something helps give you power over it.

Generativity

The analogies of a metaphor can suggest new ideas about the system (both problems and solutions). For example, we'll look at the metaphor, "Customer service is an assembly line." This suggests that a problem is handed from group to group to be worked on, but it also raises the question, "What happens when the problem gets to the end of the line? Does it just fall off?" The metaphor helps bring out important issues that might otherwise lurk and fester.

Architecture

The metaphor shapes the system by identifying key objects and suggesting aspects of their interfaces. It supports both static and dynamic aspects of the system.

Choosing a metaphor takes work. Your team should explore several possibilities, looking at the system through those metaphors' worldviews. If the best metaphor is a combination of two, that's OK.

Q&A

What if the metaphor is "wrong"? You obviously don't want this problem, but all you can do is your best. If you later realize there's a better metaphor, develop your system in that direction. This can be a very good sign: it may mean you've made a breakthrough in learning to understand your problem.

What if you can't think of any good metaphors? There's always the "naive metaphor": let objects be themselves. For example, a bank model might have Customer and Account objects. This may not give you any extra insights (because it's based on what you already know), but at least it lets you get started.

What are some system metaphors that have been used?

⋄ Double-entry accounting and a spreadsheet, combined in a pension tool [Beck, 2000, p. 56]

⋄ Desktop metaphor for graphical user interfaces [Ludolph et al., 2001]

⋄ Bill of materials in VCAPS, a car cost modeling system [*http://c2.com/cgi-bin/wiki?VcapsProject*]

⋄ Assembly line, with lines, parts, and bins, in the Chrysler C3 payroll system (the first XP project) [*http://c2.com/cgi-bin/wiki?SystemMetaphor*]

⋄ Shopping cart, for e-commerce systems. [Discussed in the e-group ExtremeProgramming]

For more information on metaphors in system design, see *Designing Information Technology in the Postmodern Age* by Richard Coyne (1995) and "A Guide to Metaphorical Design" by Kim Halskov Madsen (1994).

Example: Customer Service

Suppose we need to develop an application to support customer service representatives. For example, a customer calls to complain that long distance doesn't work on a phone. The rep takes some information from the customer, and ensures that a technician works on the problem.

We'll explore several metaphors that a team might evaluate, and see the tradeoffs we might make in letting each of these guide the system's development.

The Naive Metaphor

Customer Service Representatives create Problem Reports on behalf of Customers and assign the Reports to Technicians. In the naive metaphor, we have to carefully think through the implications of the metaphor, because it doesn't give much guidance.

Assembly Line

Think of problem reports and solutions as an Assembly Line, and the technicians and customer service representatives as Workers at Stations. This metaphor suggests that several steps or people might be needed to solve a problem.

Notice how the Assembly Line metaphor helps our understanding. For example, we might wonder how many items per hour come off the end of the line. This helps us think about the "capacity" of our operation. We might wonder what happens to an item once it hits the end of the line. Perhaps we'll want a policy of notifying each customer of the problem's resolution. We might wonder what happens when a station gets backed up. This might help us identify bottlenecks and might lead us to think of Workers as multiply skilled people who can pitch in wherever they're most needed.

Some aspects of the Assembly Line metaphor don't work so well. An assembly line tends to have a relatively fixed structure, whereas we might want something more flexible. The steps from place to place are typically predefined; we might want something that decides routing based on the situation.

Issues such as these don't necessarily invalidate the metaphor, but rather help us to explore and understand its limits.

Shared Blackboard

An Expert (CSR or technician) puts a Problem on the Board. Several Experts are sitting around: When they see a problem they can solve, or that they know how to break into easier subproblems, they do so, and write the result on the Board. A protocol defines, "Who gets the chalk next?" and "When are we done?"

This metaphor illustrates many important issues. For example, Experts have different skills and they may not necessarily agree on how to solve a particular problem. We may have "Experts" who aren't as good as they think they are. The Board may become a scarce resource. The most knowledgeable person may find he or she is doing all the work, and so on.

Subcontractors

The CSR is the General Contractor, with control over the whole Job. The CSR can let work out to Subcontractors (who can delegate to others).

This model treats the representative as a critical part of the process: the customer's advocate. Commitments and subcommitments are tracked. Time bounds (service level agreements) can be built into the contracts. Someone is always responsible overall, ensuring that problems don't fall through the cracks.

Workflow

Workflow is a generalization of the Assembly Line, to support an arbitrary graph of possible transfers, along with the idea of dynamically determining what step is next. It is in effect a semistandardized version of the naive model.

The concept of Workflow may not be a part of some people's mental framework. Even if it seems like a perfect fit based on the problem, it may not be the best choice if it won't give people any intuition about the system. (I find it a little abstract for a metaphor, but it might be just right for the right group of people.)

Conclusion

We've discussed several potential metaphors: Naive, Assembly Line, Chalkboard, Subcontracting, and Workflow. Each of these brings a different perspective on the interplay of people and problems. The team needs to consider the strengths and weaknesses of each possible model and select the best fit they can.

Example: Editors

Editors have used several metaphors and models over the years.

Card

An early editor style was to imitate punched cards: some number of lines, with 80 characters each. This was easy to implement with a simple array of characters. Users had to confront the question, "What happens when your text is longer than a line?"

Array of Lines

Other editors used another model: make each line stand on its own, with any length it needs. Again, implementation was simple: an array of pointers to variable-length lines.

String

This model was initially used by TECO and inherited by EMACS. The text is a giant string (with some character as a line separator). Lines can easily vary in length. This metaphor easily supports many operations (such as multiline searches) that could be tricky in the preceding models. See *The Craft of Text Editing* by Craig Finseth (1991).

Sequence of Runs

The previous models are adequate for simple text, but something more complicated is needed to support styles. One solution is to regard the text as a sequence of strings, each with the same style. So,

This is a **bold and <u>bold underlined</u>** <u>text</u> string.

might be encoded as:

This is a   (Regular)
bold and   (Bold)

<u>bold underlined</u>	(Bold and underlined)
<u>text</u>	(Underlined)
string.	(Regular)

Notice that each combination of styles is treated as a different run and that runs don't overlap. This metaphor gives a natural view to the meaning of selecting text and applying a style.

Tree

Another editor style is tree-based, for hierarchical data. This was common in some Lisp editors (years ago) and also used in "structure-aware" or "syntax-directed" editors. It shows up as an outline view in some editors. Today, it's a common model for editing HTML and XML; because they require properly nested tags, the nodes form a hierarchy. Tree editors have powerful operators for locating and rearranging hierarchies.

Combination

Editors often combine several modes: a tree view may be built out of a string view and vice versa. A purely tree-based editor may have simple text editing inside and so on. A combination metaphor may be best, but make sure the combined power is worth the possible confusion it may cause.

Conclusion

Each of these models has been used in real editors. The right metaphor provides the explanatory power you need, in a model that all parties understand.

More Examples

Just to give some more ideas, here are several metaphors that were brainstormed in a two-hour session, at which we considered every system we could think of (including non-XP systems).

- *Mail:* Letter, envelope, stamp, address, address book, mailbox, bank of mailboxes

- *Desktop:* File, folder, filing cabinet, trash can

- *Randomness:* Dice, wheel, cards; sampling

- *Controls and gauges:* Control panel, dashboard, knob, gauge, thermometer, probe points (special test points on a circuit board), TV remote, calibration

- *Broadcast:* Radio tower, station/channel, tuning, program

- *Time:* Clock, calendar, timer

- *Data structures:* Queue, stack, tree, table, directed graph, chain

- *Patterns:* Decorator, facade, factory, state, strategy, visitor

- *Information objects:* Book; tombstone (final report on dead process); tape recorder; bill-of-materials; knitting needle cards (cards with holes punched indicating areas of interest, collected together by sticking knitting needles through them); money sorter; music score

- *Identity:* Passport, ticket, license plate, password, lock, key, keyring

- *Surfaces:* Window, scroll; canvas, pen, brush, palette; clipboard; overlaid transparencies, menu, Lite Brite[1] screens for bitmap pictures, typewritten page, style sheet; blackboard (AI system); map; mask, skin; mirror; form; file card

- *Dynamic objects:* Outline, spreadsheet, Gantt chart, highway network

- *Connection:* Plumbing, pipe, filter; bridge; standardized connectors, adapters; plug-in modules; breadboard (components and wires); LEGO[2] pieces; puzzle

---

1. Lite Brite® is a trademark of Hasbro Inc.
2. LEGO® is a trademark of the LEGO Group.

- *Other objects:* Air mattress (compression); gate (monitor); checkpoint; glue (a la TeX word formatting); engine; toolbox; stacked camera lenses

- *Shopping:* Shopping cart, checkout

- *Notification:* Alert, alarm; lease; reservation, appointment; heartbeat

- *Processes:* Walkthrough/drive-by/fly-by; slide show; auction, bid; registration; data mining; cooking, recipe (algorithm); voting; experiment; assembly line; double-entry bookkeeping, accounting; architecture, design; pruning; balance; garbage collection

- *People:* Agent, proxy, concierge (recommendations), servant, tutor, tour guide, subcontractor

The "data structures" and "patterns" metaphors, in particular, may be a little weak to base a system around, but they are included here anyway. Some of the window-oriented metaphors are probably so folded into our consciousness as to no longer be so useful. (Twenty years ago they weren't so obvious.)

The metaphor affects how you perceive the system. Consider some of the identity metaphors: a password is changed often, whereas a key seems more permanent. Both passwords and keys are fairly anonymous. A passport, on the other hand, carries your identity and a record of where you've been.

Using Metaphors

Determine the metaphor during the exploration phase, when stories are written and spiked. Revise it as you go. Let the metaphor guide your solution. Use its names for the "uppermost" classes. Understand how those classes interact.

When I interview people, I ask them, "Tell me about the three or four key objects in your system and how they interact." (Now you're forewarned.) It used to amaze me how hard this was; many people just don't focus on what's key.

Make sure the whole team agrees on the key objects. Given three or four blank cards, would each person on the team write down the same objects?

Does the metaphor describe the problem or the solution? The solution: the key names and relationships.

Bob Koss[3] of Object Mentor says:

> I've used the metaphor to conceptually talk about a system but not to implement the system.
>
> I've used the metaphor to describe the interacting objects used to implement the system, but not to talk about the system.
>
> I've used the metaphor to both describe the system and to describe the interacting objects. This is the Holy Grail, but isn't always easily achievable.

Limits of Metaphors

It can be hard to find the right metaphor. There are several potential problems.

- The metaphor may not be familiar enough to the group that needs to use it. Double-entry bookkeeping may be the perfect metaphor, but if the accountants understand it and the programmers don't, it won't be a good system metaphor. (This may mean you need to find a new metaphor or work to make everyone understand this one, and so on.)

- The metaphor may be too weak, not powerful enough to explain the critical aspects. For example, if we're developing a distributed system, a metaphor that treats it like a simple uniprocessor may not be sophisticated enough to explain things such as network delays or failure of remote nodes.

---

3. Personal correspondence, 2001.

- A metaphor may be too strong, overshadowing but not addressing the real problem. "When all you have is a hammer, the whole world looks like a nail."

- A metaphor may unduly limit our conception of the system. Ted Nelson, of hypertext fame, argues that a spreadsheet had to be understood as a new sort of thing; in effect he argues that the metaphors provide only a shadow of its true nature (cited in Coyne 1995, p. 251). The metaphor in this case may adequately explain what the system *is*, but not what it *could be*.

- Many metaphors may be of the form, "it's like a magic xxx" ("magic typewriter," "magic paper," etc.). This is a two-edged sword. On the up side, it helps us capture some of the extra capabilities our system provides. On the down side, the point at which we need the most help ("the magic") is exactly the part that's not covered by the metaphor. Alan Kay (cited in Coyne 1995, p. 252), Bruce Tognazzini (1992), and Randall Smith (1987) discuss these issues.

Summary

We've briefly explored the meaning and usage of the system metaphor in XP.

The metaphor provides a common vision and a shared vocabulary. It helps generate new understanding of the problem and the system, and it helps direct the system's architecture.

We demonstrated how a couple of different systems might explore a variety of metaphors by brainstorming a few and comparing their worldviews.

Finally, we discussed some limitations of metaphors.

Resources

Allee, John Gage, ed. "Metaphor." *Webster's Dictionary* (publisher and year unknown).

Anonymous. 2000. "System Metaphor." *Portland Pattern Repository,* December 12. Available from *http://c2.com/cgi/wiki?SystemMetaphor.* INTERNET.

Anonymous. 2000. "Vcaps Project." *Portland Pattern Repository.* December 12. Available from *http://c2.com/cgi/wiki?VcapsProject.* INTERNET.

Beck, Kent. 2000. *Extreme Programming Explained.* Boston: Addison-Wesley.

Coyne, Richard. *Designing Information Technology in the Postmodern Age: From Method to Metaphor.* Cambridge: MIT Press.

egroups.com, on the ExtremeProgramming list. Available from *http://egroups.com.* INTERNET.

Finseth, Craig. 1991. *The Craft of Text Editing.* New York: Springer-Verlag.

Ludolph, Frank, Rod Perkins, and Dan Smith. 2001. "The Story Behind the LISA (and Macintosh) Interface." Available from *http://home.san.rr.com/deans/lisagui.html.* INTERNET.

Halskov Madsen, Kim. 1994. "A Guide to Metaphorical Design." *Communications of the ACM,* 37(12), pp. 57–62.

Smith, Randall. 1987. "Experiences with the Alternate Reality Kit: An Example of the Tension between Literalism and Magic." *IEEE Computer Graphics & Applications* (September), pp. 42–50.

Tognazzini, Bruce. 1992. *Tog on Interface.* Reading, MA: Addison-Wesley.

Part 3

Process

Chapter 7

How Do You Plan a Release? What Are Stories Like?

Write, estimate, and prioritize stories.

Release Planning

A release is a version of a system with enough new features that it can be delivered to users outside the development group. A release represents perhaps one to three months' work.

Release planning is designed to help customers identify the features of the software they want, to give the programmers a chance to explore the technology and make estimates, and to give everybody a sense of the overall schedule. The release planning process typically takes from one to a few weeks.

In Extreme Programming (XP), this process is sometimes referred to as the "Release Planning Game." It is a *cooperative* game, not a competitive one—the goal is for everybody to come out ahead. "Game" is meant in the game-theory sense, but we'll describe the process as if it were a "real" game (Cockburn, 1999).

There are two players, customer and programmers. The release planning game embeds the rights of customers and programmers into its rules. The game has tokens: the user stories, written on file cards. The game has two aspects: exploration and planning. The players can make various moves, depending on the emphasis. You can think of the game as shown in Figure 7.1.

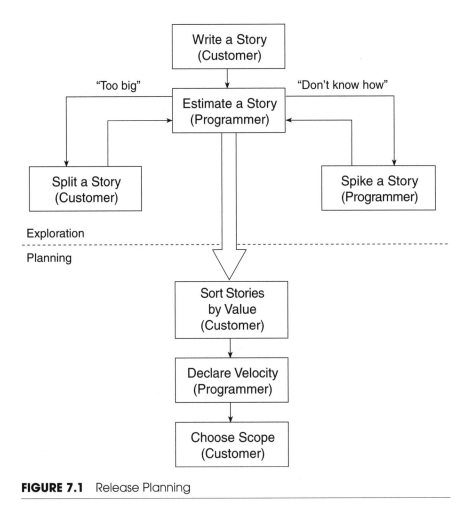

FIGURE 7.1 Release Planning

Release Planning: Exploration

Goal: Understand what the system is to do, well enough that it can be estimated.

Method: The customer writes and manages stories. The programmers estimate stories (spiking when necessary). Continue until all desired stories are estimated. Expect this to take a few days to a few weeks.

Result: A working set of estimated stories.

Activities

Customer Writes a Story

The customer captures an idea, possibly one suggested by the programmers. (Only customers should write a story and only if they want a feature.) To write a story, take a blank file card and write "Story: story title" on the top. Write a sentence or a short paragraph describing some feature of the system. Try to keep it small enough that the programmers will estimate one to three story points ("weeks").

Cite or attach supporting materials, if needed. A story card doesn't need all the details, though; it's as much a promise to discuss a feature as a description of it.

Remember that the story must be testable. The customers have to specify the tests (later on), so they should have in mind some mechanism by which to test it.

Give the card to the programmers to estimate.

Programmers Estimate a Story

The programmers try to estimate a story. (They'll probably have to ask questions, compare with previous stories, and so on.) The estimate is in ideal programmer weeks (also known as "story points"). If the estimate says it will take more than three "weeks," the programmers pass the story back to the customer to split. If the programmers don't know how to implement it, they do a spike.

Customer Splits a Story

The customer may want to split a story for more flexibility or because the programmers say it is too big for them to estimate. If the programmers want a story split, it must be split. Smaller stories tend to be less risky, so it's worth the trouble.

Take the original story card. Write two or more new story cards, each simpler than the original, that when taken together cover the original story. Rip up and throw away the original card. Give the new stories to the programmers to estimate.

Programmers Do a Spike

If the programmers don't know how to estimate something, they'll do a quick programming exploration of an issue. "Quick" means minutes to hours, to perhaps a couple of days. A spike is a skinny, minimal solution in throw-away code. The result of a spike is enough knowledge to attempt an estimate.

In the End

The customer has written stories for the desired features, and the programmers have provided each story with a price tag.

Q&A

What's this bit about story points versus weeks? Programmers usually find it easiest to estimate in terms of "ideal weeks": "If this were all I did, how long would it take?" What the programmers estimate as one week will probably take two or three real weeks to accomplish. Because these "ideal weeks" don't really exist, we can just call them story points and let everything work out from there. The exact ratio of ideal to actual weeks isn't very important, as long as it's reasonably consistent.

Release Planning: Planning

Goal: Plan the next release so it gives the most bang for the buck.
Input: Set of estimated stories.

Method: Do actions 1 through 3 below. Expect this to take up to a few hours.

Result: A prioritized list of the stories currently planned to be included in the next release (and some tentative understanding by the customer of future releases).

1. *Customer sorts stories by value.* The customer sorts from most to least valuable, or at least labeled high, medium, or low. You might think of these as "must have," "should have," and "could have."

2. *Programmers declare the velocity.* The programmers declare the velocity, that is, how many story points the customer should expect per fixed-length iteration, typically one to three weeks. The first time, a reasonable guess is one-third of a story point per programmer per week; after that, use the measured velocity.

3. *Customer chooses scope.* The customer chooses stories for the next release. To estimate how long the development effort will take, divide the total story point estimates by the velocity. For the first release, the stories must exercise the whole system end-to-end, even if at a minimal level.

Q&A

What if the customer doesn't like the resulting schedule? The customer can change the stories, release with fewer stories, accept a new date, change the team, or work with a different team entirely. The customer doesn't get to change the estimates, though.

How committed is the customer to having these stories in the chosen order? Not committed at all. The customer can change priorities at any time. The plan just gives a starting point.

Whatever happened to sorting by risk? Older descriptions of release planning described the programmers sorting the stories by risk. Many teams don't bother with this; most of the risk seems to show up in longer estimates, so the sorting is redundant. I recommend that a team think about ways to reduce risk in longer stories, but allow the customer to choose the order of the stories.

Example

We'll demonstrate release planning—exploration and planning—in an example. First, we need some sort of overall vision for the system.

> *Vision*
>
> *Produce a system able to search an electronic library card catalog.*

We might hope for a little more on why we want to do this and how we think our system will be better than others, but it's a reasonable starting point.

Exploration: Writing and Estimating

The release planning game begins when the customer starts writing stories. They write a card:

> *Story: Query=>Details*
>
> *Given a query, return a list of all matching items. Look at the details of any items.*

The programmers look at this story and try to estimate it, but they come back and say, "It's too big." The customer says, "Let me split it into a few cards," writes some new ones, and throws the original away.

> **Story: Query**
>
> Query by author, title, or keyword.

> **Story: Z39.50**
>
> Use Z39.50 (the ANSI standard for searching library catalogs).

> **Story: Any Format**
>
> Support any document format.

The programmers say, "We can't estimate for *any* format; which ones are most important?" The customer rips up the "any format" card and writes two others.

> ### Story: MARC
>
> Support Z39.2 MARC document format (ANSI standard).

> ### Story: SUTRS
>
> Support simple text document format (SUTRS) (from Z39.50).

The customer says, "There might be other formats later, but we'll start with these."

The programmers will estimate the stories. We'll assume they have some familiarity with Z39.50 and the ASN.1 protocol it uses. But they may decide to do a quick spike: they already have a tool to handle the protocol encoding, so one pair might attempt to do a simple "login" connection to a Z39.50 system. Another programmer might research the MARC format, and code up a quick tool to parse a record. Someone else might look at SUTRS. Another pair might try to encode a simple query. (With luck, the programmers will have been able to do some of this investigation before the planning game, or part of the team may have been hired for expertise that can take most of the issues into account.)

After the investigations, the programmers say, "Queries: two weeks; Z39.50: three weeks; MARC: two weeks; SUTRS: one week." (Note that these are really "story points," and may represent more than that many weeks of programmer effort.) Meanwhile, the customer has been coming up with more stories.

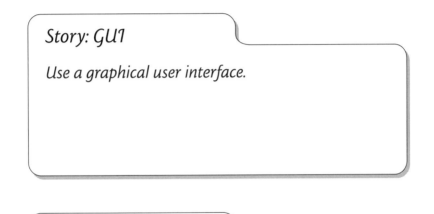

Customer: "We'd like a graphical user interface so it's easy to use."

Programmers: "For what you've described so far, two weeks."

Customer: "Not all library systems can sort, but we'd like to take advantage of those that can."

Programmers (after some quick investigation): "Two weeks."

Story: Drill-down

Z39.50 systems can let you look at either quick information (e.g., title, author, year) or the whole record. Instead of always showing the whole record, drill down from quick results to individual items.

Programmers: "Two weeks."

Story: No-drill for 1

Don't make me drill down if the result has only one item.

Programmers: "One week."

Story: Save Results

Save search results to a file.

Programmers: "What's this for?"

Customer: "It lets other programs see the results; the user can share the file with friends, use it in a document, and so on."

Programmers: "One week."

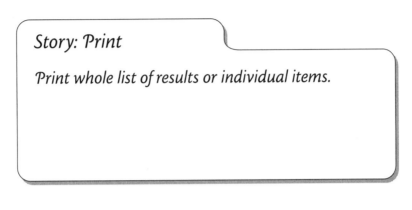

Story: Print

Print whole list of results or individual items.

Programmers: "Two weeks."

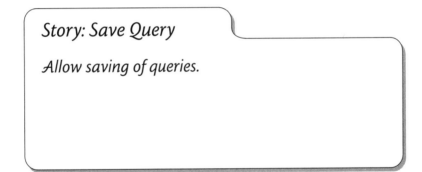

Story: Save Query

Allow saving of queries.

Programmers: "How is this different from saving the results?"

Customer: "You won't get the same result every time even if you search with the same query."

Programmers: "What?!?!"

Customer: "Libraries buy new books every day. Some people like a standing query that they can run just to see what's new."

Programmers: "Oh, OK. One week."

> *Story: Booleans*
>
> *Support Boolean queries ("and," "or," and "not").*

Programmers: "Three weeks."

> *Story: Config*
>
> *Configure what library we're working with.*

Programmers: "What kind of configuration information do we need?"

Customer: "It's similar to a URL on the Web: host, port, and database name. Many users just use the same library all the time, but others use a variety. We'd like the users to be able to have a list of libraries."

Programmers: "Two weeks."

Programmers: "How about a few more stories: one about what types of systems we should run on and one about performance?"

Customer: "Good idea. Here you go." (Notice that the programmers can *suggest* that this type of story be added, but it's up to the customer to write it, and the customer can reject the suggestion completely.)

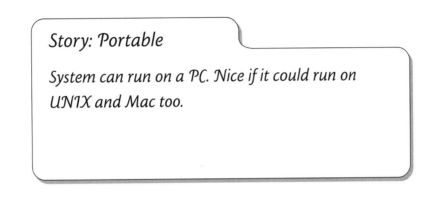

Programmers: "Our programmers are familiar with C++ and Java, and both of those could be used. Here are some trade-offs . . . [*Mercifully omitted*]. If you want to go with C++, we'll need to split the story because the system-specific parts will make it take longer than three weeks. If you're willing to go with Java, we estimate one week [to arrange for multiple machines and development and testing environments]."

> ### Story: Portable (Java)
>
> *System can run on a PC. Nice if it could run on UNIX and Mac too.*

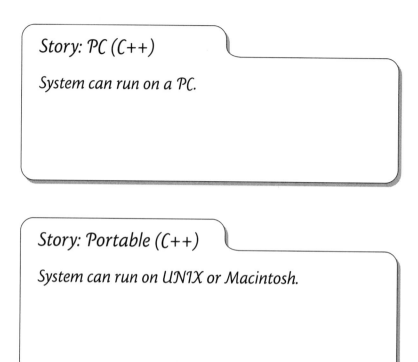

Story: PC (C++)

System can run on a PC.

Story: Portable (C++)

System can run on UNIX or Macintosh.

Programmers: "So, Portable (Java) costs one point; PC (C++) costs two points; and Portable (C++) costs two points as well."

Customer: "We'll take Java." They rip up the two C++ cards. Notice that the programmers estimated the costs of the two technologies, but the decision is the customer's. This is only fair; the customer is the one who has to pay to support it going forward.

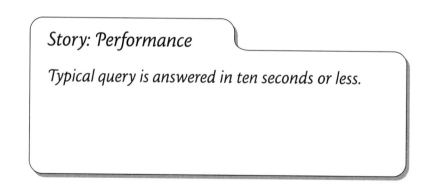

Story: Performance

Typical query is answered in ten seconds or less.

The programmers do a quick spike, using a "quick" GUI and a simplified system. It appears that the bulk of time is spent waiting on the network. They tell the users, "One week." (This allows for some time to establish a performance monitoring tool and for performance tuning.)

Planning: Sorting and Selecting

The customer sorts the stories by value (Table 7.1). The estimate is in parentheses.

The programmers say, "The velocity is five, meaning we expect to deliver five estimated points per three-week iteration with our team."

The customer says, "I know we need a minimally functioning system as soon as possible. These are the stories I think we'll need for the first release." (Table 7.2.)

Notice that this is all the high-value items and selected medium-value items. At five story points per iteration, this will take about three iterations.

TABLE 7.1 Sorted Stories

Value	Stories
High	Z39.50 (3)
	Query (2)
	MARC (2)
	GUI (2)
	Performance (1)
Medium	Boolean (3)
	Sorting (2)
	Drill-Down (2)
	SUTRS (1)
	Config (2)
	Portable (1)
Low	Print (2)
	No-Drill (1)
	Save Result (1)
	Save Query (1)

TABLE 7.2 Release Plan

Story Points	Story Name
3	Z39.50
2	Query
2	MARC
2	GUI
1	Performance
1	SUTRS
2	Config
1	Portable

Next, development can proceed (beginning with iteration planning). We'll look at iteration planning in the next chapter.

Summary

We have:

◇ Described the release planning process, as embodied in the planning game

◇ Explored, by writing and estimating a number of stories

◇ Planned, by sorting and selecting stories for the release plan

Resources

Beck, Kent, and Martin Fowler. 2001. *Planning Extreme Programming*. Boston: Addison-Wesley.

Cockburn, Alistair. 1999. "Software Development as a Cooperative Game." Available from *http://members.aol.com/humansandt/papers/asgame/asgame.htm*. INTERNET.

Chapter 8

How Do You Plan an Iteration?

Iteration planning can be thought of as a board game.

The goal of iteration planning is to take the stories a team plans to implement in the iteration (the stories currently most valuable to the customer), break those stories into smaller tasks, and assign programmers to work on the tasks.

Rather than producing everything in a "big bang" at the end, an Extreme Programming (XP) team uses a series of iterations. Iterations are of a fixed length, one to three weeks long. Iterations are time-boxed: if the team can't get everything done, they will drop features rather than slip the end-date of the iteration. At the end of each iteration, the customer should expect to see the system ready to deliver, running the acceptance tests for the stories you've chosen.

On the first day of each iteration, the team will decide on which stories they'll focus. Just as release planning used a game (over weeks), the iteration planning process uses a game too. It typically requires perhaps one to four hours, because this planning covers a much smaller amount of work. The iteration plan will identify what tasks will be done over the next one to three weeks and who will do them.

The team accomplished some number of story points in the previous iteration; the customer can select that many points worth of story cards for the next iteration. The stories don't have to be in the order they were in for the release plan; the customer can request them in any order. In fact, the customer may introduce new stories if the customer is willing to give the team time to estimate them.

To help understand the process, you can think of iteration planning as a board game. There are tokens (story cards, task cards, and coins) and "squares" to move them in. The board and rules are as shown in Figure 8.1.

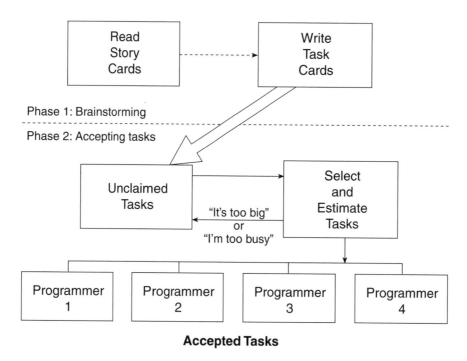

FIGURE 8.1 Iteration Planning Game

Setup

⋄ The tracker (see Chapter 9) reminds the team how many story points ("weeks") were completed last iteration. This is the "Yesterday's Weather" Rule: the past is your best prediction for the future. On the first iteration, the team should make its best guess; as a default, assume one-third story point per programmer per week.

⋄ The customer selects the unfinished stories desired, provided the total story points fit that limit.

⋄ The tracker reminds the programmers how many task points ("days") they completed in the last iteration. On the first iteration, assume one-half task point per programmer per day in the iteration. Be aware that programmers' task points will tend to vary more than the team's story points.

⋄ Each programmer puts that many coins in his or her Accepted Tasks box. (Different programmers will have different numbers of coins.)

Phase 1: Team Brainstorms Tasks

In the brainstorming phase, read each story card and work with the team to brainstorm the tasks it might involve. At the end of this phase, the programmers will have a pile of task cards, corresponding to the story cards the customer has selected. (A given task may support many stories.)

⋄ The customer picks a story card and reads it aloud.

⋄ The programmers brainstorm the tasks required to implement that story. (This will usually involve discussions with the customer.) They write a task card for each task identified.

⋄ The process continues until each story card has been read.

⋄ The stack of task cards is moved to the Unclaimed Tasks pile.

Phase 2: Programmers Accept Tasks

The accepting phase of the game is mostly the programmers' job. They will individually select the tasks they prefer, estimate them, and accept the ones they agree to perform. In addition to conversations to clarify what is needed, the customer may be involved in this phase for two reasons:

 ✧ If the programmers can't fit in all the tasks, they'll ask to defer or split a story.

 ✧ If they have more time than tasks, they may ask for another story.

So:

 ✧ For each task, some programmer will select it, estimate it in task points ("days"), and write the estimate on the card in pencil.

 ✧ If the task is bigger than three days ("too big"), the team can split the task and put the new tasks on the Unclaimed Tasks pile.

 ✧ If programmers have fewer coins than their estimate ("too busy"), they erase their estimate and return the card to the Unclaimed Tasks pile.

 ✧ Otherwise, programmers can accept the task by removing as many coins as their estimate and adding the card to their stack.

 ✧ This all happens in parallel as various programmers claim various tasks.

 ✧ Continue until the team gets stuck, needs more stories, or wins.

Finishing

One of three things will happen: the team will have too much to do, too little to do, or just about the right amount.

Team Gets Stuck (can't find a way to win)

- ✧ The customer picks a story to split or defer.

- ✧ For a split story, brainstorm new tasks. For a deferred story, remove the corresponding tasks.

- ✧ Phase 2 is tried again.

Team Needs More Stories

- ✧ There are programmers who haven't used up all their coins, but the tasks are all claimed.

- ✧ The customer can add in another story and see if the team can fit it in.

Team Wins

- ✧ All tasks are accepted.

- ✧ The workload is reasonably balanced (everybody has approximately 0 coins left).

Next

By the end of the game, the team has developed an iteration plan that should enable them to implement the stories.

- ✧ The manager may record the iteration plan.

- ✧ Customers start writing acceptance tests.

- ✧ Programmers implement tasks.

Q&A

How long should this take? Perhaps a few hours.

Why do we have to identify tasks anyway? Aren't the stories good enough? Some teams just keep the stories small and use them directly, but others find it helpful to identify tasks. Tasks are easier to estimate than stories because they're smaller. One task may support multiple stories, so there are some advantages to having both.

Do we really have to use the game board and task cards? No, of course not. The game board is just a diagram to remind you how the iteration planning process works. Many teams don't bother to create cards for tasks; they use explicit cards for stories, but just track tasks on a whiteboard so they can be checked off in public view as they're completed.

Why should the customer have to split or defer a story if the team gets stuck? If the team did so many story points last time, why can't they do that many this time? The estimate for the story was just that: an estimate. After the team has taken the trouble to break it up into tasks and estimate those, they have better information about the actual work involved.

But won't that make the team's schedule slip? The release plan said this story could be done. It might well affect the schedule. You hope there are other stories that come in quicker than you asked to make up for it. If not, at least you know now.

Is the sum of the task points equal to the story points? No, it's not necessarily so. It will depend how you estimate them. If you're reasonably consistent, it will all work out.

How do you know who gets which task? In XP, programmers choose their tasks, rather than management assigning them. There may be a little jostling, but the team should be able to devise its own system.

But what if a programmer wants to do the wrong kind of task (e.g., a GUI programmer wants to do a database task)? XP's natural instinct is to avoid specialization, so this cross-training is actually a good thing. Remember, this programmer will have a pair partner and can work with someone who has experience in the area. Also, the programmer's inexperience will tend to be reflected in his or her task estimate (higher than an expert might say for the same task).

Does a programmer own a task, or does a pair own a task? Programmers own tasks as individuals; a programmer might use several different pair partners in the course of getting the task done.

Why doesn't the whole team estimate the tasks? Shouldn't the team's best estimate stand? (After all, that's the way you estimate stories.) This is a key difference between release planning and iteration planning. One way to think of it: "The team owns the story, the programmer owns the task; therefore, the team owns story estimates, but the programmer owns task estimates." There's a psychological reason as well: you're more likely to accept an estimate you made for your own work than an estimate the team assigned to you.

Another reason is that personalized estimates can be more accurate. Suppose Alice finished five task points last iteration and Bob finished ten. It's possible they're equally productive, but just have a different estimation style. Neither estimate, nor their average, is necessarily right for an arbitrary person on the team. If a programmer estimates consistently and produces consistently, his or her estimates will converge to the right number over time.

How do we ensure that when we put the tasks back together we've covered the whole story? The customer will be writing acceptance tests for the story; this will tell you whether the story is done. If the team is missing tasks that complete a story, the tests will show it. The team will have to cover them somehow and adjust the schedule if necessary. Some teams give each story an explicit owner.

How can a programmer know how long to estimate for a task? The programmer can talk to the customer or other programmers, compare the task to previous task estimates, do a quick spike (5 to 60 minutes), or go with a number that "feels right."

Can a programmer make contingent estimates (e.g., "one day if Jan helps me, otherwise three days.")? Sure. Just make sure Jan is willing to play it that way, and don't let things get too complicated.

Summary

- ✧ The customer selects the stories for the iteration.

- ✧ The team brainstorms what the tasks are, but individual programmers estimate and accept them.

- ✧ Use the "Yesterday's Weather" Rule for both story points and task points.

- ✧ The team may have to do some juggling.

Resource

Beck, Kent, and Martin Fowler. 2001. *Planning Extreme Programming.* Boston: Addison-Wesley.

Chapter 9

Customer, Programmer, Manager: What's a Typical Day?

Customer: Questions, tests, and steering
Programmer: Testing, coding, and refactoring
Manager: Project manager, tracker, and coach

Assume we've been through release planning and iteration planning. What happens in a typical day during an iteration?

Customer

As a customer of Extreme Programming (XP) software, you will sit with the team full-time to write tests, answer questions, and set priorities. Having the customer with the team is crucial in helping the team go as fast as possible.

I once worked with a cross-functional team that had moved into one large room for a key project. In the "lessons learned" session, a manager in the marketing group said he thought the experience was great, because he was answering questions right when they came up and he could see the progress resulting from his answers. He admitted that when he was back in his office, he'd get a voicemail, but put off answering for a day or two. (Meanwhile, the developers either made a guess or worked on something less important.)

It takes many decisions to develop software. If a team can get its answers or decisions in minutes instead of hours or days, its speed will be much higher.

XP is not the only approach that recognizes the value of an on-site customer. Tom Peters says, "Make clients an integral part of every project team" (Peters, 1999, p. 105) and "If the client won't give you full-time, top-flight members, beg off the project. The client isn't serious" (ibid., p. 106).

The customer has four key jobs during the iteration:

1. Answer questions

2. Write acceptance tests

3. Run acceptance tests

4. Steer the iteration

and one job (after several iterations) when the release is ready:

1. Accept the release

Answer Questions

One of the main reasons you're an on-site customer is so you can answer questions for the programmers while they're implementing tasks.

When asked a question, answer right away if you can or promise to find out (and do so quickly). This feedback cycle of minutes instead of hours or days is one of the key things that lets an XP team move quickly.

Many questions are not questions of fact: they require you to make a decision. Your decisions are important: they're how you get what you need. For example, if you've said you want some data cleaned up, the programmers may present you with options, but you have to tell them which one you want.

Once you've answered a question, you'll want to keep track of your answer. The best way to do this is to write an acceptance test or (more rarely) write a story.

Write Acceptance Tests

For each story in the iteration, determine what would make you confident that the story was properly implemented and write a test to verify it. Progress in the iteration will be measured against the tests, so the sooner they're available, the better.

In the simplest form, a test will be a card with the title "Test: test-title FOR story-title," containing information about the test. In a better case, you may be able to specify the test in a spreadsheet; you will want to spend some story or task points to get a tool to run these tests automatically. Also, you may have a programmer or tester who will help: you specify the test, and the programmer or tester will implement it. Be aware that if you require a programmer to work on the tests, this will affect the number of story points the person can deliver.

Software testing is a discipline unto itself; a good starting point would be Kaner et al. (1999) or Beizer (1995).

When you're designing tests, think about the input and the expected result (you need to capture both). Test both what should happen when things are right, and what should happen when they go wrong. For example, a word processor test might specify what happens when the disk is full. It can also be revealing to have tests that are at a boundary condition and on either side of it. For example, if you're allowing numbers 1 to 9999, try 0, 1, 2, 9998, 9999, and 10000 as test values. (There's certainly a lot more to testing than this brief introduction.)

Try to keep your tests fairly independent of each other. When one test breaks, you don't want a chain reaction with too many problems to examine. If tests are independent, you can run them in any order, without a lot of setup.

Acceptance tests are crucial: they're your "gauge" so you can measure how good the program is.

Run Acceptance Tests

Every day, run the acceptance tests for all stories expected to be implemented by the end of the iteration. Let the team know which tests pass and which fail. The manager (tracker) will keep a graph where everybody can see it. After you run these tests by hand for a few days, you'll see why you will prefer automated tests.

By the end of the iteration, you want like all tests to pass, although it won't necessarily be so.

Steer the Iteration

You have three key opportunities to guide the team:

- *Release planning:* You choose what's in, what's out, and the release date.

- *Iteration planning:* You choose what stories are in each iteration.

- *On the fly (within the iteration):* You choose what the team does *right now.*

There will be times when you need to adjust the plan. Perhaps the development team is not progressing as quickly as planned, and they need to drop some features for the iteration. Given the team's progress, *you* are best able to decide which story is more crucial or whether a story can be meaningfully split.

Or there may be a change in business conditions. Perhaps marketing has identified a killer feature that would enable sales to book many orders if only it were available by the show date. In this case, you can introduce the new story, get it estimated, and reprioritize the team's activities. You prefer not to interrupt an iteration in progress if you can avoid it, but if you ask, the team will set aside or throw away what they've done and devote themselves to the new features. Do a new release plan whenever you need to.

Accept the Release

As you get closer to release time, the programmers will be handling the final tasks of installing the software. Once they're ready, you'll want to run the acceptance tests one last time, along with whatever else you need to be sure the software is ready to go live.

When the software is in and you're satisfied, take a deep breath and declare, "We accept the release." Notify anybody who needs to know.

A release is a big deal; celebrate with the team, then relax and explore a little before jumping in to the next release.

Q&A

But I've got a job to do. How can I spend all my time with this team? Well, hopefully it won't have to be *all* your time. You'll probably be able to do a little work other than this, but this is definitely an investment. Fortunately or not, an on-site customer is the best person to guide an XP team, by deciding what to do, setting priorities, and answering questions.

Can't I just talk to analysts and let them translate what I want? XP has no analyst role per se; the customer works directly with the programmers. XP strives for the high-bandwidth communication of having the person with the problem talk directly to someone who might be able to solve it.

What if there are many customers? The development process needs input that is prioritized into a single stream of requests. The potential customers need to find a way to trade off their particular requirements.

What if there are many, many *customers?* "Customer" is a role; there may be product managers or marketing people who can stand up and make the necessary *business* decisions.

Programmer

XP is unusual as methodologies go, in that it prescribes activities at the day-by-day (and even at the minute-by-minute) level. We can think of XP's programming activities as shown in Figure 9.1.

The triangle in the middle of Figure 9.1 captures the idea of test-first programming, a key feature of XP:

✧ Test, then code, then refactor

This is the opposite of traditional programming, which does

✧ Design, then code, then test

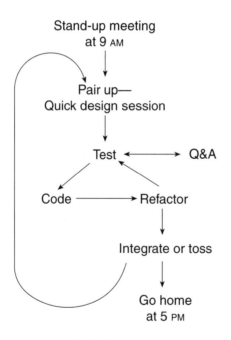

FIGURE 9.1 XP Programming Activities

In traditional programming, the cycle might take weeks to months; in XP, the cycle happens on the order of minutes to hours. Let's look at the activities one at a time.

Stand Up Meeting at 9 AM

⬥ Meet for 10 minutes at the beginning of the day.

⬥ Identify problems and who will solve them, but don't try to solve them in the meeting.

⬥ Fix the starting time; this helps remind the team to work a 40-hour week.

Pair Up and Do a Quick Design

⬥ All production code is produced by a pair.

⬥ The typist thinks tactically, the partner thinks strategically.

⬥ Switch roles periodically.

Test

⬥ Write only small bits of unit-test code at a time.

⬥ Verify that the test fails before coding. (It's sure interesting if it doesn't fail.)

⬥ "Test everything that could possibly break."

⬥ Ask the customer if you're not sure what the answer should be.

Code

⬥ Implement just enough to make the tests pass. ("Do the Simplest Thing That Could Possibly Work.")

⬥ Follow the team's coding standard.

Refactor

- ✧ Seek out "code smells" (places that don't feel right); apply a refactoring; verify that the unit tests still pass.
- ✧ The code should:
  - Run all unit tests
  - Communicate what it needs to communicate
  - Have no duplicate logic
  - Have as few classes and methods as possible
- ✧ Take small steps, and unit-test after each.
- ✧ See *Refactoring* (Fowler et al., 1999).

Q&A

- ✧ The customer is available on-site to provide immediate answers.
- ✧ Many questions require decisions (not facts), and the customer should be prepared to make them.
- ✧ The customer should write an acceptance test or (more rarely) a story to capture the answer.

Integrate or Toss

- ✧ Move the code to the integration machine, build the system, and run all tests.
- ✧ Fix things to bring the unit tests back to 100 percent.
- ✧ Some teams require that acceptance tests be in no worse condition. (No test that was passing before you got there should be failing now.)
- ✧ If you can't easily integrate, throw it away and try again tomorrow.

Return to "Pair Up"

- If you have time left in the day, you can pair up (or at least switch roles) and start over on another task (perhaps the partner's).

Go Home at 5 PM

- Going home on time reinforces the practice of having a 40-hour week.
- Notice that nothing is hanging over your head: everything you've done for the day is integrated or tossed.

Summary

These activities remind you of important aspects of XP:

- Always have a partner.
- Get answers before you code.
- Program test-first.
- Throw it away when you need to.
- Go home "clean."

Manager

There are three prominent roles in managing XP:

- (Project) Manager
- Tracker
- Coach

The *manager* owns the team and its problems. The manager presents a face to the world, forms the team, obtains resources, and manages people and problems.

The *tracker* helps the team know if it's on track for what it's promised to deliver. This typically is not a full-time role.

The *coach* helps the team use and understand the XP approach, mentors the team, and helps the team get back on track if it goes "into the weeds."

Depending on the size of the team, all three roles might be embodied in one person or in several. A team of moderate size will want separate people, because it can be emotionally hard to be both manager and coach.

What Doesn't an XP Manager Do?

If you're a manager of an XP team, there are several things you won't do, that a typical project manager might under some other discipline.

✧ You don't set priorities; the customer does that.

✧ You don't assign tasks; programmers do that.

✧ You don't estimate how long stories or tasks will take; programmers do that.

✧ You don't dictate schedules; the customer and programmers negotiate them.

What's left? That's what we'll explore.

What Does an XP Manager Do?

The manager has several key jobs: face outside parties, form the team, obtain resources, manage the team, and manage the team's problems.

Face Outside Parties

As a manager, you will deal with several parties. The first is "funders": a manager needs resources (including money) to manage. The manager provides the funders with insight into the results of their spending. If a manager can't convince someone to support the team, there will be no team.

You will deal with customers. The customer is the person (or group) willing to claim responsibility for setting priorities and choosing functionality. This may be a user or user surrogate; it could be (but often isn't) the funder. XP requires an on-site customer who will make critical decisions. An XP manager needs to set the customer's expectations appropriately: the team needs a knowledgeable and committed customer.

You will interact with other people as well. This will include people internal to the company (e.g., database administrators) or external groups (e.g., salespeople or specialists).

Form the Team

The manager assembles the team of programmers (through hiring, transferring, or contracting). If you're forming an XP team, the programmers need to know that at the beginning. The manager will help the team bond and help to establish its process. Ideally, especially for a larger team, the team will include a coach.

Obtain Resources

The manager must obtain resources for the team.

You need to create a team workspace. XP values face-to-face communication as the highest-bandwidth way to share knowledge. An open workspace reinforces communication. This space needs to be set up to allow people to pair-program. (This doesn't fit the usual corporate model of cubes.) Most teams will want at least some "personal space" as well.

The team needs hardware and software with which to program. Some teams dedicate a machine to integration and release. Other teams simulate this with a physical token (although it's a lot easier to forget to grab the stuffed animal than to forget to move to the standard machine).

Your team won't be experts at everything: at some point, they may ask you to obtain specialist consulting. XP teams regard specialists as a resource for their learning. Rather than expecting an expert to do a job, it wants the expert to teach the team to do the job.

You'll need miscellaneous office supplies: paper, pens, markers, and of course file cards. (Like anything, you can delegate this job, but the ultimate responsibility is yours.)

Manage the Team

The manager has several responsibilities centered around the team:

Report Progress. The funder, and possibly many other groups, care about the progress and status of your team. Track risks and issues so those people have the information they need.

Host Meetings. You'll handle the logistics for meetings: making sure there's a place to meet, that everyone knows about it, that supplies are available, and so on. The key meetings are the release planning meeting, the iteration planning meetings, and the daily stand-up meetings. You may find you need other meetings as well, but don't let "meetings" get in the way of "work."

Host Celebrations. You have many opportunities to celebrate what the team does: release plan complete, iteration complete, system released, or other important days. Handle the logistics: make sure the right people are invited and that the team gets the celebration it deserves.

Manage Problems

As a manager, you'll face problems. (XP doesn't change *everything*.)

A project may hit a crisis of some sort. The manager needs to be in the loop, ready to deal with the customer or even the funder. The attitude is not "Woe is me," but rather "This is something you need to know," hopefully followed by "Here are some offers we can make to help it get better."

A team will hit roadblocks that don't quite reach the crisis level. There may be places where your authority can get something done in minutes that would take the programmers days or weeks. Perhaps it's in dealing with a troublesome outside team, purchasing software, or solving an environment problem. If even you can't make headway, you may need to get the customer involved.

Sometimes the problem will be a troublesome member of the team: you may have to get rid of a team member who refuses to follow the team's rules.

If there are outside distractions, the team should minimize these where it can and find a way to deal with them where it must. Production support is an example; you might sacrifice someone to an iteration if he volunteers for pager duty.

If there is outside pressure, remember that the customer is in the hot seat for setting priorities; deflect such pressure away from the programmers.

Tracker

The tracker handles the mechanics of measuring the team's progress. (Some teams combine the tracker with the manager.)

The tracker can act as a disinterested party, with little "skin" in the game. This is a strength. I've been in positions in which I've been 95 percent tracker and 5 percent programmer. It amazes me how much having one task on the tracking list interferes with my perception of the priority and status of the others.

There are three basic things the tracker will track: the release plan, the iteration plan, and acceptance tests. You can easily make simple spreadsheets for the tracking you need to do.

You may find other things to track as well. If you can measure a problematic but controllable behavior, the very act of putting up a chart will tend to improve it. Don't overburden yourself though: remove such a chart once it has served its purpose.

Track the Release Plan (Stories)

In release planning, the customer decides the order of stories and which ones are planned for the release. In its simplest form, this information can be maintained in two stacks of cards, those "in"

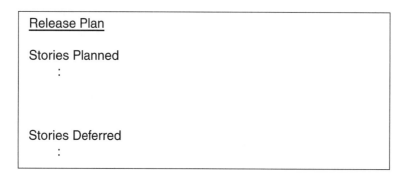

FIGURE 9.2 Release Plan Chart

(planned for the current release) and those "out." Or you may want a chart as a more permanent record (Figure 9.2).

The release plan probably won't change radically more often than every few iterations, so it's not a big burden to track this information.

Track the Iteration Plan (Tasks)

The iteration plan covers a shorter time period, but requires more active tracking. Recall that iteration planning will identify the stories and tasks to be completed in an iteration.

Creating the iteration plan requires some critical information: how many story points did the team complete, and how many task points did each programmer complete, in the previous iteration. (It's your job to track and supply that information.) Again, you might maintain this information on cards, on a whiteboard, or in a chart (Figure 9.3). (Note that one task may support many stories.)

During the iteration, at least a couple of times a week, you'll talk to the programmers individually and find out how many task points they've spent on a task and how many remain until completion. You might get this information during the daily stand-up meeting. You can use this information to decide if a team is on track for the iteration. If you're on the middle Monday morning of a two-week iteration, but fewer than half the tasks are done, raise a flag. With luck, the team

```
┌────────────────────────────────────────────────────┐
│  Iteration Plan                                    │
│  ──────────────                                    │
│                                                    │
│  Iteration: N      Start date    End date          │
│                                                    │
│  Story: Task  Task  Task  ...                      │
│  Story: Task  Task  Task  ...                      │
└────────────────────────────────────────────────────┘
```

FIGURE 9.3 Iteration Plan Chart

can adjust internally. If not, the team may have to ask the customer to adjust the plan by deferring or splitting stories.

Acceptance Tests

The tracker will maintain a chart for the acceptance tests (the tests defined by the customer). Normally, the customer or a tester will actually run the tests. You might make a table, but the information is far more compelling as a poster in graph form (Figure 9.4).

As the days go by, you want to see more tests in total and fewer failed tests. If that's not the case, people will notice.

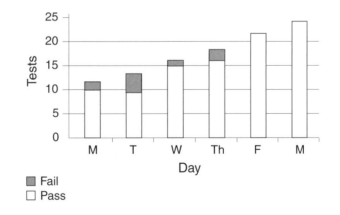

FIGURE 9.4 Acceptance Tests Graph

Coach

The coach role evolved as someone "on the ground" to help the team maintain its process. Alistair Cockburn (2001) describes XP as a "high-discipline" process, and the coach is one of the tools XP uses to maintain that discipline. We'll look at the attributes and activities of a coach and some problems a coach might face.

Attributes

The coach should be a mature person. "Calm" is too passive a description; it would be more accurate to say a coach should be "centered," unflappable, not easily fazed. The ones I've known (XP or not) have all been good, even expert, programmers. (And the team seems to sense that if they really need it, the coach can go deep into the well for something to help.)

A coach is respected, but also respectful. He or she is willing to talk, but also willing to listen. The coach lets the team explore, but provides a guardrail in case of danger.

Finally, the coach is on-site. Just like the customer must be there to answer questions, run tests, and set priorities, the coach is there to mentor, monitor, and help.

Activities

The coach's activities focus on the process and the team. The coach will tend to own few or no development tasks.

Monitor the Process. The coach's key job is to monitor the process. If stand-up meetings become two-hour affairs, people are skipping unit tests, acceptance tests are not being written, or people are consistently leaving late, the coach needs to blow the whistle. Usually, just calling attention to a problem is enough to wake people up to solving it.

Enforce the Process. On occasion, you get someone who purpose-fully does not follow the team's rules. This can't be allowed to continue; it can destroy the team's productivity and morale.

Ron Jeffries (Jeffries, 2001), the coach on Chrysler's C3 project, describes his approach:

> What I do (as opposed to how I talk) is that when someone is transgressing rules in some way, I'll have a talk with them. Usually something bad will have happened, which lets us begin by agreeing that something bad shouldn't happen again. I relate the rules to the bad effect in an impersonal way:
>
> The UnitTests weren't run before the code was released. The UnitTests would have shown the problem. That's why we insist on running them every time. We're fallible, the computer isn't.
>
> Usually the problem won't occur again. Also I watch the person and nag them a few times in a friendly way.
>
> Perhaps most importantly, I'd coach the other team members to watch out for the bad behavior when partnering. In other words, gang up on him.
>
> If it does happen again, I'll have a still friendly but serious chat that says "Everyone in the group really does have to follow the rules." Since they're programmers, they can do the math on people who don't follow the rules.
>
> If it happens a third time, I would politely but gently remove them from the group. If removing them isn't possible, I'd make it turn out that they didn't get to work on anything important. [...]
>
> Extreme Programming (and leadership in general) is a work of love. If you don't respect others, you're not doing it right. I try always to let my great respect show through for people who try hard to do the right thing. And sure enough, they do try, in almost every case. The others, who are perhaps trying in some way I don't understand... I respect them too... and wish them success elsewhere.

Change the Process. One of XP's rules is "They're just rules": sometimes, the best thing to do is change a process. The coach can help the team spot these areas and work through to a new approach.

Mentor. The coach is available for mentoring. This may be to work as a design partner or programming pair, or to help someone find their way on a subject new to them.

Supply Toys. The coach may see that the team needs a reminder about something, and a toy may be just what's needed. Or a toy may be needed to give the team permission to relax a little.

Problems

In addition to keeping the process in line, the coach will be sensitive to problems that might arise. Here's a sampling:

Velocity Slowing Down. The tracker may report that the team is completing fewer task points or story points than planned. If there are no obvious reasons (a hurricane shut down the building, lots of family emergencies, etc.), the team needs to do some soul-searching: are they refactoring? producing all the tests? pairing? and so on.

Messy or Duplicate Code. This is a sign that refactoring is not being done well or often enough. The team needs to be reminded that the "simplest" code requires work to keep it that way. In a bad case, the team may have to take some time just for refactoring.

Quality Going Down (as measured by the tests or difficulty integrating). The team needs to focus more on testing "everything that could possibly break." See if you can identify a particular type of error that seems to be slipping through and devise a test approach for it.

Summary

We've looked at three roles in managing XP:

1. *Manager:* Face outside parties, form the team, obtain resources, manage the team, and manage problems.

2. *Tracker:* Track the release plan, track the iteration plans, track acceptance tests.

3. *Coach:* Monitor, enforce, and change the process; mentor; supply toys; handle problems.

A team may organize these roles as needed, but you should ensure that each of these areas is addressed.

General Summary

We've looked at three roles: customer, programmer, and manager, and what they do during an iteration. The customer guides current and future development; the programmer focuses on the code; and the manager acts as project manager, tracker, and coach.

Resources

Beck, Kent. 2000. *Extreme Programming Explained.* Boston: Addison-Wesley.

Beck, Kent, and Martin Fowler. 2000. *Planning Extreme Programming.* Boston: Addison-Wesley.

Beizer, Boris. 1995. *Black-Box Testing: Techniques for Functional Testing of Software and Systems.* New York: John Wiley & Sons.

Cockburn, Alistair. 2001. "Just in Time Methodology Construction." Available from *http://members.aol.com/humansandt/papers/jitmethy/jitmethy.htm.* INTERNET.

Fowler, Martin, Kent Beck, John Brant, William Opdyke, and Don Roberts. 1999. *Refactoring: Improving the Design of Existing Code.* Reading, MA: Addison-Wesley.

Jeffries, Ron. 2001. Available from *http://c2.com/cgi/wiki?EnforcingMethods.* INTERNET.

Kaner, Cem, Hung Quoc Nguyen, and Jack Falk. 1999. *Testing Computer Software, Second Edition.* New York: John Wiley & Sons.

Peters, Tom. 1999. *The Professional Service Firm 50.* New York: Alfred A. Knopf.

Chapter 10

Conclusion

How Rigid Is XP?

Extreme Programming (XP) is not as inflexible as I've made it sound throughout the book. Kent Beck's "Twelve Practices" are a starting point, but XP will change in each environment.

There's a caution though: if you drop the open workspace (your facilities won't allow it), the on-site customer (they're too busy), the pair programming (we don't like it and we're in two locations anyway), and so on, you can find yourself thinking you're doing XP without really getting all its possible benefits.

XP asks a team to be "awake," thinking about what works and what doesn't and looking for ways to improve.

What Does XP Tell Us That We Already Knew?

XP tells us several things:

⋄ *High-bandwidth communication works.* If you get people in one room, where they can make decisions and see results, you can speed things up immensely.

- *Validation is important.* XP reduces the time from having an idea, to defining its validation criteria to completing its implementation. By requiring automated, repeatable tests, the team is sure it is moving forward.

- *Iteration works.* Iteration is not a new concept, but many teams that claim to be iterative are not. XP forces iteration by prescribing multiple integrations per day, one- to three-week long iterations that deliver a working system, and releases every few months.

What Is the Next Big Skill?

The market will go to those who have big visions but who can get there through small releases.

- Identify and implement 90 percent solutions.

- Break stories into easy and hard parts.

- Know what's important and what's not.

Where Is XP Going?

Yogi Berra once said, "It's hard to make predictions, especially about the future." I'll make some guesses anyway.

- *Simplification and clarification:* The planning process still seems more complicated than it has to be. How to integrate continuously is probably not explained well enough. The metaphor idea is powerful, but many teams aren't using it.

- *Limits of XP:* Can a large team do XP? Can it apply in this domain or that? When and where is XP the right thing to do?

- *Search for underlying values:* The XP community has been exploring whether there are underlying principles that can inform those using other methods.

- *Acceptance tests:* XP uses automated acceptance tests generated by the customer. I think we'll see a burst of energy as people face what this means in different environments.

- *Customer role:* We've mostly focused on the programmer's view of XP. ("Give me a bunch of easy stories to work on, answer all my questions, and give me a bunch of tests so I know when I'm done.") It's hard to be a customer of software, and I think there will be many more ideas on this subject.

How Do I Get Started with XP?

If you think XP would be good for your team, but the team doesn't see XP as part of its shared vision, you have a classic problem of influencing others to try something that *might* be good but is *definitely* different. Remember the onion analogy in the Introduction:

- Some things you can do on your own: test-first programming, refactoring ...

- Some things require the programmers to work together: pair programming, collective ownership, coding standard ...

- Some things require the customer to work with the programmers: planning game, small releases ...

You don't have to start with all of XP on the first day; your team must develop its own process.

If your team has a consensus that XP is what it wants, this book and others will help you. Web sites are available, and there are discussion groups happy to talk to you. There are companies that do training in XP and ones that will supply a coach or mentor for your team. Good luck—you're in for a lot of fun.

Bibliography

Extreme Programming

Anonymous. 2000. "Extreme Programming Roadmap." *Portland Pattern Repository* (December 12). Available from *http://c2.com/cgi/wiki?ExtremeProgrammingRoadmap*. INTERNET

Beck, Kent. 2000. *Extreme Programming Explained.* Boston: Addison-Wesley.
> The original book describing the XP process, and you won't want to miss it. It describes the philosophy of XP, and gives overviews of all the core practices.

Beck, Kent, and Martin Fowler. 2000. *Planning Extreme Programming.* Boston: Addison-Wesley.
> Planning, in detail.

Fowler, Martin, et al. 1999. *Refactoring: Improving the Design of Existing Code.* Reading, MA: Addison-Wesley.
> The mechanics of how to improve code. The core of the book is a catalog of step-by-step refactorings, shown in Java.

Jeffries, Ron, Ann Anderson, and Chet Hendrickson. 2000. *Extreme Programming Installed.* Boston: Addison-Wesley.
> Tells how the C3 team at Chrysler used XP. It begins with "The Circle of Life," describes clear customer and programmer roles, and continues running strong on how the practices are used.

Good Stuff

Cockburn, Alistair. 1998. *Surviving Object-Oriented Projects*. Reading, MA: Addison-Wesley.

Highsmith III, James A. 2000. *Adaptive Software Development: A Collaborative Approach to Managing Complex Systems*. New York: Dorset House.

Hunt, Andrew, and David Thomas. 2000. *The Pragmatic Programmer: From Journeyman to Master*. Boston: Addison-Wesley.
   Lots of good advice from programmers who've been there.

Classics

Bentley, Jon L. 1982. *Writing Efficient Programs*. Englewood Cliffs, NJ: Prentice-Hall.

———. 1988. *More Programming Pearls: Confessions of a Coder*. Reading, MA: Addison-Wesley.

———. 2000. *Programming Pearls, Second Edition*. Boston: Addison-Wesley.

Brooks, Fred. 1985. *The Mythical Man-Month*. Reading, MA: Addison-Wesley.

DeMarco, Tom, and Timothy Lister. 1987. *Peopleware: Productive Projects and Teams*. New York: Dorset House.

Gamma, Erich, et al. 1995. *Design Patterns: Elements of Reusable Object-Oriented Software*. Reading, MA: Addison-Wesley.

Knuth, Donald E. 1968. *The Art of Computer Programming*. 3 vols. Reading, MA: Addison-Wesley.

Slow Going

Coyne, Richard. 1995. *Designing Information Technology in the Postmodern Age*. Cambridge, MA: MIT Press.
   Metaphors and multiple viewpoints.

Lakoff, George, and Mark Johnson. 1983. *Metaphors We Live By*. Chicago: University of Chicago Press.

Schön, Donald. 1990. *The Reflective Practitioner.* New York: Basic Books.

Testing

Beizer, Boris. 1995. *Black-Box Testing: Techniques for Functional Testing of Software and Systems.* New York: John Wiley & Sons.

Kaner, Cem, Hung Quoc Nguyen, and Jack Falk. 1999. *Testing Computer Software, Second Edition.* New York: John Wiley & Sons.

For Fun

The Princess Bride. 1987. Hollywood: MGM.

Tolkien, J.R.R. 1999. *The Hobbit, or There and Back Again.* Boston: Houghton Mifflin (originally published in 1937).

Web Sites

news:comp.software.extreme-programming

http://www.egroups.com/group/extremeprogramming

http://www.extremeprogramming.org—Don Wells' site

http://www.junit.org—JUnit's home

http://www.pairprogramming.com

http://www.refactoring.com—Martin Fowler's refactoring catalog

http://www.xpdeveloper.com

http://www.xprogramming.com—Ron Jeffries' site

http://www.xp123.com—Bill Wake's site

Index

A

Acceptance tests, xx, 119, 145
  graph, *137*
  running of, by customers, 126
  tracking of, by trackers, 135, 137
  written by customers, 124, 125–
    126, 130
"Anti-patterns," 27
Architecture, 75–83
  defined, 75
  documenting, 81
  Extreme Programming, xxiv
  first iteration, 76, 78–79, 83
  4+1 View Model, 75
  metaphor, 76, 77, 83, 86
  refactoring, 76, 80–81, 83
  small releases, 76, 80, 83
  spike, 76–77, 83
  team practices, 76, 81, 83
Array of lines model, 90

Arrays
  refactoring, to convert to
    Vector, 14, 17
Assembly line metaphor
  customer service example, 88

B

Beck, Kent, xiv, xxiii, 4, 7, 27, 55,
  78, 81, 85, 143
Beizer, Boris, 125
Berra, Yogi, 144
Black box, 48
Brain
  paired programming and
    nature of, 70
Broadcast metaphor, 92
Bug-fixing
  refactoring separated from, 32
Bugs, 82
Builds, daily, 52–53

Note: Italicized page locators indicate figures and tables.

Bullpen office type, 57
Bus number, 50

C

Capital One, 64, 70
Card metaphor, 90
Case sensitivity, 13
Celebrations
    and XP managers, 134
Chrysler 3C project, 139
Coaches
    role of, in managing XP, 132,
        138–140, 141
    See also Customers; Trackers
Cockburn, Alistair, 82, 138
Code
    breaking, 53
    duplicate, 29, 140
    testable, 3
    unit test, 129. *See also* Refactoring
"Code freeze," 52
Code ownership, xxiii, 47, 48–52,
    60
    collective, 50–52
    by layer ("tribalism"), 50
    monogamous, 48–49
    orphan, 48
    "serial monogamy" or "rental
        property," 49–50
    "tag," "musical chairs," or "trial
        by fire," 48
Code reviews, xxiv
    and paired programming, 70
Code smells, 27, 30, 31, 42, 43,
    130
Coding standards, xxiii, 47, 59–60,
    81, 129, 145

"Coding wars," 56
Collective code ownership, 50–52,
    145
Combination metaphor, 91
Configuration
    and first iteration, 79
Connection metaphor, 92
Contingent estimates, 121
Continuous integration, 53
Controls and gauges metaphor, 92
Coyne, Richard, 87
Cross-training, 82, 120
Crowd programming, 64
Cubicles, 56
Customers, xiii, xx
    acceptance tests written by, 130
    and Extreme Programming, xx,
        xxi–xxii
    future role of in XP, 145
    and paired programming, 65
    and planning game, xxiv
    questions and answers by/for,
        127–128
    and release planning, 99
    and Release Planning Game, 100
    role of, during iteration, 123–128
    scope chosen by, 103
    stories selected for iteration by,
        117, 122
    stories split by, 102
    stories written by, 101
    tasks of, during release planning,
        135–136
    and XP managers, 133
    See also Coaches; Programmers;
        Trackers
Customer service example, 87–89

D

Daily builds, 52–53

Data

    denormalization, 48

    model, 82

"Data bag" class 7

Data structures metaphor, 92, 93

DeMarco, Tom, 56

Deployment (technical) architecture, 81

Deployment view, 75

Design, xxiii, 5–7

    metaphors in, 87

    and paired programming, 70, 72

    in test-first programming, 129

    of tests, 125

Desktop metaphor, 87, 92

Disengaged programming, 64–65

"Do It" interface, *58*, 79, *80*

Domain objects, 6

"Do the Simplest Thing That Could Possibly Work" principle, 10

DRY ("Don't Repeat Yourself") principle, 30

Duplicate code, 29, 140

Dynamic objects metaphor, 92

E

E-commerce

    shopping carts for, 87

Editors example, 90–91

"Eight-hour burn," 54

EMACS, 90

Empty queries, 13

Examples

    customer service, 87–89

    editors, 90–91

more metaphors, 91–93

release planning: exploration, 104–113

release planning: sorting and selecting, 113–114

Extract Method, *28*, 31, 34, 35, 43

Extreme Programming, 26

    and architecture, 75–76

    and coding standard, 59, 60

    collective code ownership used by, 51–52

    description of, xiii, xix–xxii

    and 40-hour work week, 54–55, 131

    future of, 144–145

    getting started with, 145

    layered approach with, x

    limitations with, 83, 144

    open workspaces specified by, 56

    as processes, xxiv

    as programming, xxiii

    programming activities, *128*

    resources, xxv

    rigidity and, 143

    small releases favored by, 58

    as team practices, xxiii–xxiv

    test/code cycle in, *8*

    underlying values in, 144

    See also Team practices

F

Finseth, Craig, 90

Firewalls, 78, 79

First iteration, 76, 78–79, *80*, 83

"4+1 View Model of Architecture, The" (Kruchten), 75

40-hour work week, 54, 55, 60, 131

    See also Workspaces

Fowler, Martin, 23, 27, 28, 32, 81, 130
Functionality
    and first iteration, 79
Funders
    and XP managers, 132–133, 134

G

Gamma, Erich, 4
Generativity
    and metaphor, 86
Geographically separate groups, 55–56
Getter tests, 7
Graphical user interfaces, 20, 58
    desktop metaphors for, 87
    test-first programming for, 16
GUIs. *See* Graphical user interfaces

H

Hardware, 133
Heart
    paired programming and nature of, 70–71
"Hello, world" program, 78–79
High-bandwidth communication
    effectiveness of, 143
Hill, Michael, 59, 78
Hosting meetings
    and XP managers, 134
Hunt, Andy, 30

I

"Ideal weeks"
    and story points, 102
Identity metaphor, 92, 93
Implementation view, 75
Incremental programming, 3

Information objects metaphor, 92
Integration, xxiii, 47, 60, 130, 133, 144
    continuous, 53
    daily builds, 52–53
    just before delivery, 52
Interfaces
    one-button, 79, *80*
    See also Graphical user interfaces
Iteration plan/planning, 114, 115–122
    chart, *137*
    and customers, 126
    as a game, 116–119
    goal of, 115
    tracker and tracking of, 135, 136–137
    See also Release plan/planning
Iterations, xiii, 115
    first, 76, 78–79, *80*, 83
    importance of, 144
    typical day during, 123–141
    and "Yesterday's Weather" Rule, 54

J

Java programming language, xiv
Jeffries, Ron, 139
JUnit framework, 4–5, 27

K

Kaner, Cem, 125
Kay, Alan, 95
Keyboard
    and paired programming, 69
Kirk, Harris, 70
Koss, Bob, 94
Kruchten, Philippe, 75

L

Layered code ownership ("tribalism"), 50
Leadership, 139
Lee, Stan, 27
Lister, Timothy, 56
Logical view, 75

M

Madsen, Kim Halskov, 87
Mail metaphor, 92
Managers
    role of, in managing XP, 131–135, 140
Martin, Bob, 54
Meetings
    and XP managers, 134
Mentoring
    and coaches, 140
Metaphors, xiv, xxiii, xxiv, 76, 77, 80, 83
    customer service example, 87–89
    defined, 85
    editors example, 90–91
    limits of, 94–95
    naive, 6, 87, 88
    seeking, 85–86
    in system design, 87
    using, 93–94
Metsker, Steve, 54, 64
Model
    test-first programming in development of, 5
Monogamous code ownership, 48–49
"Musical chairs" code ownership, 48

N

Naive metaphor, 6, 87
    customer service example, 88
Nelson, Ted, 95
Notification metaphor, 93

O

Object Mentor, 94
Object-oriented (OO) programming, xi
Offices
    one- or two-person, 56
    supplies for, 134
One-button interfaces, 79, 80
On the fly (within the iteration)
    and customers, 126
Open workspaces, 56–58, 60, 81, 133, 143
    example of, 57
Orphan code ownership, 48
Other objects metaphor, 93
Overtime, xxiii, 47, 53–54, 60

P

Painter-Wakefield, Christopher, 72
Pair programming, xxii, xxiv, 63–73, 81, 133, 143, 145
    and collective code ownership, 51
    counter-examples, 63–69
    ensuring success of, 71
    true pairing, 65–69
    why it works, 70–71
Parameterize Method, 36
Partners, 69, 129, 131
    See also Pair programming
Patterns metaphor, 92, 93
People metaphor, 93

Personalized estimates, 121
Peters, Tom, 124
Planning games, xxiv, 145
Polymorphism, 27
Problem management
    and XP manager, 134–135
Problem solving
    by coaches, 140
Process
    and role of coaches, 138–140
    view, 75
Processes metaphor, 93
Productivity
    and paired programming, 69
Programmers, xxiv, 125
    coaches as, 138
    and Extreme Programming, xx,
        xxi–xxii
    iteration planning tasks accepted
        by, 118
    and Release Planning Game, 100
    role of, during iteration, 128–
        131
    spikes done by, 102
    stories estimated by, 101
    and task estimates, 121, 122
    and task ownership, 121
    velocity declared by, 103, 113.
    See also Coaches; Customers;
        Trackers
Programming
    Extreme Programming as, xxiii.
    See also Extreme programming;
        Pair programming; Test-
        first programming
Programs
    writing, 3–20
Progress reports, 134

Q
Questions
    answered by customers, 124–125

R
Randomness metaphor, 92
Rational Unified Process, 82
    architecture in, 75
    metaphors in, 77
    and Software Architecture Doc-
        ument, 81
Readers, 38, 41
Refactoring, xiii, xxiii, 14, 17, 23–
        43, 76, 80–81, 83, 130, 140,
        145
    analysis of, 41–42
    and architecture, 80–81
    and bug-fixing, 32
    catalog of, 28–29
    and code ownership by layer, 50
    code smells, 27
    coding standard support for, 59
    and collective code ownership,
        50, 51
    defined, 23
    final result of, 39–41
    and monogamous code owner-
        ship, 49
    original code, 24–25
    and paired programming, 66
    process, 29–30
    sample, *28*
    unit tests, 26–27
Release acceptance
    by customers, 127
Release plan/planning, xxiv, 99, *114*
    chart, *136*
    and customers, 126

exploration, 101–102
planning, 102–103
tracker and tracking of, 135–136
See also Iteration plan/planning
Release Planning Game, xxiv, 99, *100*
   exploration: writing and estimating, 104–113
Releases, xiii, xx, xxiii, 144
   defined, 99
   and Extreme Programming, ix
Release schedules, xxiii, 47, 60
   small releases, 58–59
"Rental property" code ownership, 49–50
Resources
   XP manager and gathering of, 133
Risk
   sorting by, 103
RUP. *See* Rational Unified Process

S

Sales interface, simple, *80*
Schedules
   crunches, 54
   and iteration planning, 120
Scope
   chosen by customers, 103
Screen-scraping technology, 48
Search client
   public methods, *19*
Searcher, 5
   and document loading, 16–19
Searcher class, 11–15, 20
   public methods, *19*
Search system
   user interface for, *6*

Sequence of runs metaphor, 90–91
"Serial monogamy" code ownership, 49–50
Setter tests, 7
Sharing blackboard metaphor, 88–89
Shopping cart, 87
Shopping metaphor, 93
Simple design, xiv
Skinny versions of system, 78, 82
Small releases, 60, 76, 80, 83, 144, 145
Smith, Randall, 95
Software, 133
Software Architecture Document, 81
Software development
   Extreme Programming approach to, xx–xxii
   traditional approach to, xix–xx
Software testing, 125
Solo programming, 63–64
"Spidey-sense," 27
Spikes and spiking, 76–77, 80, 81, 83, 101, 102, 121
Stories, 144
   estimating, by programmers, 101, 106, 107, 108, 109, 110
   sorting, by customers, 103, 113
   splitting, by customers, 102
   writing, by customers, 101
Story cards, 101, 102, 116
   for exploration: writing and estimating, 104–111
Story estimates
   ownership of, 121

Story points, 101, 117, 120
  and "ideal weeks," 102
  in iteration planning, 116, 117
  and velocity, 103
Struct classes, 27
Subcontracting metaphor, 89
Substitutions, 34–37, 41
Subteams
  and code ownership by layer, 50
Surfaces metaphor, 92
Switch statements, 27
Synchronization, 82
System metaphor, 85–95

T

"Tag" code ownership, 48
Task cards, 116, 120
Task estimates
  ownership of, 121
Task identification
  reasons for, 119–120
Task ownership, 121
Task points, 118, 120
Team formation
  and XP managers, 133
Team management
  and XP managers, 134–135
Team practices, xix, 47–60, 76, 81,
    83
  code ownership, 47, 48–52
  coding standard, 47, 59–60
  Extreme Programming as, xi-xii
  integration, 47, 52–53
  overtime, 47, 53–55
  release schedule: small releases,
    47, 58–59
  workspaces, 47, 55–58

Teams, xiii
  and getting started with XP, 145
TECO, 90
Telecommuting, 55–56
Templates
  representing, 31, 41
Test/code cycle
  in XP, 8
testEmptyResult( ) method, 15
Testers, 125
Test-first approach, 3
Test-first programming, xiv, xxiii,
    26, 128, 145
  for graphical user interfaces, 16
  in model development, 5
  for user interfaces, 16
Testing, xix, xxiii, 140
  code changes alternated with,
    29
  and Document, 7–9
  and Extreme Programming, viii
  software, 125
Thomas, Dave, 30
Threading, 82
Time metaphor, 92
Time zones
  and geographically separate
    groups, 55
"To do" list, 13
Tognazzini, Bruce, 95
Trackers, 117, 140
  and acceptance test runs, 126
  role of, in managing XP, 131,
    132, 135–137, 140
  See also Coaches; Customers
Tree editors, 91
"Trial by fire" code ownership, 48

"Tribalism," 50
"Twelve Practices," 143

U

Unit-test code, 129
Unit tests/testing, 29, 42, 130
   and collective code ownership,
      51
   pattern for, 4
   in refactoring, 26–27
Use Cases, xix
Use-case view, 75
User acceptance tests. *See* Accep-
    tance tests
User interfaces
   for search system, *6*
   test/code cycle for, 16
User stories, 100

V

Validation
   importance of, 144
Velocity, 140
   programmers and declaring of,
      103, 113
Vision
   and metaphor, 85–86, 95
   for release planning, 104
Vision Statement, xix

VisualAge for Java (IBM), 8
Vocabulary
   and metaphor, 86, 95

W

Web servers, 78, 79
Williams, Laurie, 69
Workflow metaphor, 89
Workspaces, xxiii, 47, 55–58, 60
   cubicles, 56
   geographically separate, 55–56
   offices, 56
   open, 56–58, 133, 143
Writing programs, 3–20

X

XP. *See* Extreme Programming
"XPlorations," xv

Y

YAGNI ("You Aren't Gonna Need
    It") rule, 82
"Yesterday's Weather" rule, 54,
    117, 122
Yourdon, Edward, 54

Z

Zero Feature Release ("ziffer"),
    59, 78

The XP Series

Kent Beck, Series Advisor

*Extreme Programming
Explained*
By Kent Beck
0201616416
Paperback
© 2000

The XP Manifesto

*Planning Extreme
Programming*
By Kent Beck and
Martin Fowler
0201710919
Paperback
© 2001

Planning Projects with XP

*Extreme Programming
Installed*
By Ron Jeffries, Ann
Anderson, and Chet
Hendrickson
0201708426
Paperback
© 2001

**Get XP Up and Running in
Your Organization**

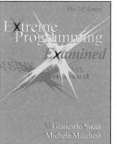

*Extreme Programming
Examined*
By Giancarlo Succi and
Michele Marchesi
0201710404
Paperback
© 2001

**Best XP Practices as Presented and Analyzed at
the recent Extreme Programming Conference**

*Extreme Programming in
Practice*
By James Newkirk and
Robert C. Martin
0201709376
Paperback
© 2001

**Learn from the Chronicle of an
XP Project**

*Extreme Programming
Explored*
By William C. Wake
0201733978
Paperback
© 2002

Best XP Practices for Developers

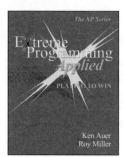

*Extreme Programming
Applied*
By Ken Auer and Roy
Miller
0201616408
Paperback
© 2002

Delves Deeper into XP Theory

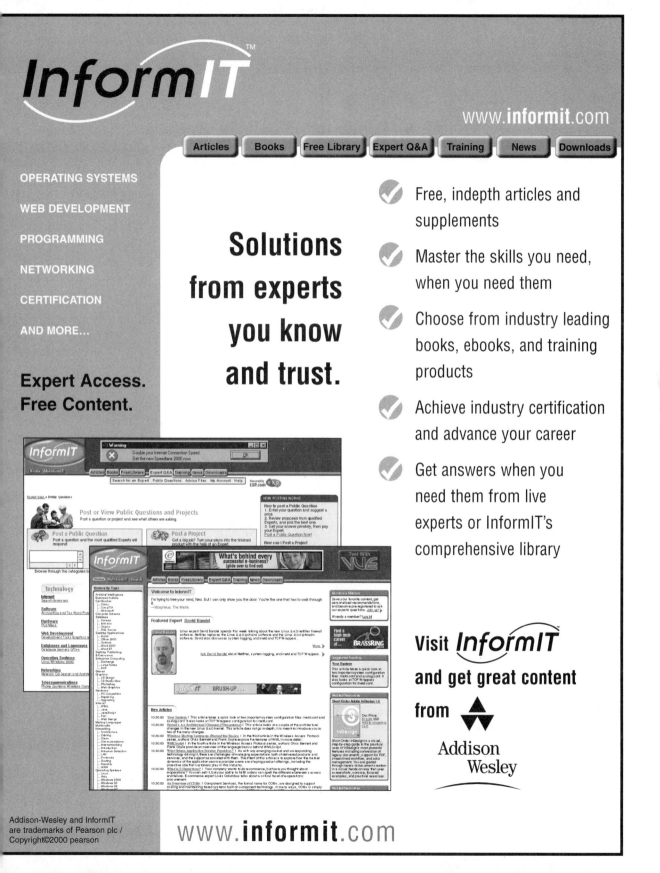